WISDOM OF THE GUARDIAN

Treasures From Archangel Michael to Change Your Life

Dr. Joy S. Pedersen

iUniverse, Inc.
Bloomington

Wisdom of the Guardian
Treasures From Archangel Michael to Change Your Life

iUniverse books may be ordered through booksellers or by contacting:

iUniverse
1663 Liberty Drive
Bloomington, IN 47403
www.iuniverse.com
1-800-Authors (1-800-288-4677)

ISBN: 978-1-4502-9703-5 (pbk)
ISBN: 978-1-4502-9704-2 (cloth)
ISBN: 978-1-4502-9705-9 (ebk)

Printed in the United States of America

iUniverse rev. date: 3/3/2011

We dedicate this book to our Divine Creator.

And, to all those who wish to experience heaven on earth; this book was written for you.

This book is filled with light, love, and blessings that will help raise the vibration of the reader to help them transition into the life they were meant to have if they choose it.

Archangel Michael, Angel of Most High

Contents

Foreword
by God

Dear Reader:

Michael the Archangel has come a long way to give you these messages. I believe you will enjoy and benefit from Michael's book. It serves all of humanity.

Trust is very important and all of his messages are about My truth. Time is of the essence. It is important for all to adhere to the words.

I love you all.

"I am" the "I am", "I am" the "I"

Acknowledgments

Michael, I am honored that you chose me to deliver this book for you. Thank you for making it relatively easy. I am blessed to be your representative and have you walk with me daily. I appreciate you guiding, assisting, protecting and defending me. Life has certainly been more interesting and fulfilling since I became conscious of your participation in it.

Whether it was encouragement, emotional support, or editing, typing and proofreading, I want to acknowledge Andrea Miller, Candace Warren, Carl Worner, Irina Smirnova, Linda Cutrupi, MaryAnn Ruggiano, Rev. Oreste D'Aversa, Geoff Steck, and Sande Foster for their contributions in helping me complete this project.

Preface
by Joy S. Pedersen

As a teenager, I was fascinated by the occult, saw the occasional ghost, believed in reincarnation, played with Ouija boards and read books on spiritual topics.

In 1979 I moved to Los Angeles and was introduced to and studied metaphysics, and I learned how to recall past lives. My goal was to get a job at a movie studio and I ended up working in network television at Paramount Studios in the PR department on shows such as *Happy Days, Cheers, Taxi* and *Family Ties*. While there, people asked me how I got my job and it made me realize that many were struggling to find their desired work, where I had not. I couldn't figure out what set me apart, so I ventured to learn what made the difference. I began to study success and found that my positive attitude and my natural ability to network were significant factors. I eventually launched my business, Express Success, providing seminars, workshops and consultations to help others succeed. The techniques I shared were the same I used to create everything in my life, including my career, business ventures and other opportunities.

When I left the entertainment industry, I was Bureau Chief of the syndicated television show, *PM Magazine,* where I was responsible for the celebrity stories that were featured. Although I loved living in Los Angeles and working in television was fun, I had the desire to make more of a difference in the world. I ended up returning to my home state of New Jersey where I began teaching a seminar entitled *The Art of Networking* and running networking groups. I was making a difference in the lives of others in many ways, but still felt more of a spiritual calling.

Applying the same steps to success for everything I wanted worked effortlessly in some areas, yet in others there seemed to be more difficulty.

The challenges I had in achieving optimal results were overcome by a process I learned in 1986 called ho'oponopono, an ancient Hawaiian spiritual process that was updated by Morrnah Simeona. Ho'oponopono was the missing link that I began to apply to every area in my life with wonderful results, but I kept the work to myself. Because of my ability to see past lives, I also began to see the cause of problems that may have stemmed from other lives and karmic situations, and I gained a better understanding of how to apply ho'oponopono to solve problems. "Clearing" is the term I use for the ho'oponopono method of ridding yourself or others of blockages that stop the natural flow of positive spiritual energy.

One of the benefits that I enjoyed by clearing using the ho'oponopono process, was that I became more aware. My morning meditations were providing answers to questions I had about my own life as well as circumstances at large. I would receive useful guidance that sometimes included pages of information. Then, I kept receiving the message, "It will soon be revealed who you are." At the time, I couldn't understand this revelation, but I was intrigued.

It was finally revealed that I was an angel who had been incarnated this lifetime for a purpose. The spiritual calling I felt was emerging because the time had arrived when mankind was more ready to accept it. Thus began a major shift in the experiences I had, as now I became conscious of angels, ascended masters and others visiting me and sharing their messages. On occasion, I had seen angels, but I didn't give much thought to them one way or another. Now, with this revelation, I could have been knocked over with one of their feathers!

As time went on, Michael the Archangel became a steadfast regular, and others appeared according to circumstances or needs at the time. Until their appearance, I didn't know all that much about angels. I was familiar with Bible stories where angels spoke to and guided people thousands of years ago. My interest was certainly piqued, so I started to read about the various angels and their areas of specialty. I hadn't even realized how popular Michael was across the major religions. The angels provided me guidance as to situations, issues to clear, and recommendations regarding everything from personal to business matters.

Isaiah, who some may recall from Bible stories, offered his services to me in business, but most remarkably showed up one night warning me to clear with earth changes. He said I would not be personally affected by the changes that would come to pass, but he had an urgency about having me clear with them. I later learned that an earthquake occurred nearby that evening that would have been worse had I not followed the instructions given to me that night.

On another occasion, just after a networking luncheon, I received a visitation from a Hindu goddess, Lakshmi, who came to assist in clearing my home and recalibrating it and me to attain greater abundance. Goddesses weren't part of my conscious awareness either. I had no idea they actually existed. As I'm relating this, I realize that these stories might sound farfetched to most people, but to me they have now become commonplace. I realize there are a lot of things I wasn't taught to believe as I was growing up but my experiences now show me that these things are real.

One day, Archangel Michael asked me to write his book of 22 chapters, which I did using automatic writing when I felt inspired. My affinity for automatic writing was born when I watched a morning television talk show in the early '90s called *The Other Side*. One morning, the show featured a segment on automatic writing and I experimented with it by following the instructions given during the show. After 18 pages, I realized I had written something that I couldn't interpret but it was clear to me that it had meaning because of the experience of writing it and the way I felt during the exercise. That began my interest in using this technique when I meditated.

Each day Archangel Michael provided another chapter in a most effortless manner. When I had received and written Chapter 22, I felt I had completed his message but I realized that it was only the beginning of the real work. I had this wonderful manuscript in my hands and didn't want to tell anyone about it for fear of ridicule.

Other than the handful of friends that shared my spiritual interests, I rarely mentioned my experiences to anyone. I did a lot of spiritual clearing on world events and problems that others and I had experienced, but I would do so in silence. I was frustrated about feeling that I had to keep this wonderful manuscript a secret. I had to look within to see what stopped me from sharing it with others. My ability to review past lives allowed me to see why I didn't want to tell anyone of these experiences.

My previous lives spent in the public eye or lifetimes as a psychic or healer, only seemed to cause me pain – persecution, imprisonment, disfigurement or death. There wasn't a big win in repeating those paths, so it was no wonder I kept quiet.

On an intellectual level, I knew how outrageous and ridiculous my experiences would sound to the average person. The more I cleared, however, the more comfortable I became with sharing those experiences. The easier it was, the more I shared. When I found myself stumped again, I knew there was more to clear. As I cleared, I found I told others about what I experienced more effortlessly. I rationalized that I was hesitant to share what I did because I operated in the business community and I would appear odd and I feared losing credibility and business opportunities. Eventually, I realized the cause of my fear and cleared it until I felt compelled to deliver the messages I was receiving regardless of the outcome. The more comfortable I became, the more I was able to follow my mission and guidance. The astonishing thing to me was that as I started sharing the information with the business community, they wanted to hire me to help them overcome their obstacles.

Now I have come almost full circle from my initial years of training in metaphysics and business offerings under Express Success. I am helping individuals and businesses using the tools of ho'oponopono, my past life insights, and the guidance of God, angels and others. I was guided to use the titles of spiritual healer and messenger before I was comfortable with them. I actually became an ordained minister, certified spiritual health coach, licensed spiritual healer and completed my doctorate to help present this work. However, I know that ho'oponopono clearing had more to do with my ability to perform, share the work and help people with it, than any of my subsequent education.

So, my dilemma about keeping my spiritual experiences private was finally overcome and I am happy to be able to share Archangel Michael's book with all of you. I have transcribed the words as Archangel Michael dictated them to me. Sometimes the writing style is a bit awkward, but the message is strong and true. I am honored that through me, Michael is sending his message of salvation to the world.

As I followed my guidance to share the messages that I received on my blog at www.AngelEnlightenment.com, it became easier and easier to tell my story. As with those messages, I was able to reread this book time and again, and gain something from it with each reading. As I also stated on the blog. I hope these messages, like those, will help you as much as they have helped me.

Joy

P.S. Great News! As we go to press, Archangel Michael has informed me that he has another book he wishes me to write when I am ready. He is definitely way ahead of me, but I'm excited and looking forward to sharing it with you.

Introduction

I am Michael the Archangel. I am the angel of the Most High, created at the beginning of time to be the Protector of God's purpose, empire, and position. I fiercely protect God and all of His creations. I am depicted by sword and by shield, each of which serves a purpose. They are not just ornamentation.

Take my guidance, as I have God's will as well as your best interests in mind. I have come at this time out of salvation for mankind. I am with you now to help you transition into the new world of heaven on earth, and that peace lay supreme for all.

People struggle, search, and reach out to me for answers, while the answers lie within.

I am here to serve you; however, often you do not need my help. All you need do is look to the I within. He is there to answer your every need; your every whim. I am here also, but you should not just rely on me. The I, your Source, is within you, each and every one of you. The same source lies within me as well. I am another vehicle to reach the Source but you do not need me. You can access the Source directly each and every time you feel you need to connect, you need an answer, you require a solution, or just want comfort.

You have traveled a long and arduous path. You have struggled, wandered, returned, given up, gotten up, excelled, failed, rejoiced, fought, cried, laughed, smiled, won, lost, and on and on, over and over during the course of your existence. You have done none of it alone. We have all been with you, and the Source, without a doubt, has never left you. You may have left Him, but He has never left you.

But the search goes on, the questioning abounds. The doubts permeate your very existence. You wonder whether or not you believe in something greater than you or are you just fooled into believing in something that may or may not *really* exist. We hear your cries, your doubts, your questions, and your wondering whether or not there really is a God. You cry and blame Him when something goes wrong. You laugh and cry when something goes right and you feel lucky. Nothing in either of those situations is different other than your lack of perception as to who you are, what your role is, and the impact your thoughts can have on a situation.

What troubles me is that you miss the point. The point keeps getting drummed home over eons of time, but you continue to miss the point. The point is *you are responsible for your life and its outcome. You can make the difference in your life and its outcome.* None of you are victims of circumstance. Each and every one of you has created the circumstances within which you live. You have either created them before you arrived here on this planet to learn a specific lesson in your spiritual growth, or you chose them once you arrived by default, by lack of correct thinking, or by the actions that you've taken.

At no other time in history have the decisions made by mankind over eons of time been more prevalent. The reason is that this is the time when all is to be brought into balance. All is to be brought into right thinking, right action, and right being. All of you have the choice to become one with the Source and live rightly or pay the consequences of not learning those right actions.

There is more struggle and inner turmoil today than ever before regarding the outer expression of those thoughts and feelings that dominate your mind. I will not sit still any longer and watch you struggle and blame others, most of all your Creator, and scramble and search outside of yourself looking for answers that lie within, which you keep missing. You are too close to the situation, so you keep looking outside yourself, while the answers lie within. They also lie in your circumstances if you look at them. *Look at them!* You have created them. Why do you suppose you created them? *To learn something.* The purpose is to learn something from the mirror you place before your eyes, reflecting the circumstances you have created in order to understand yourself better. That is all.

You have a choice in each moment of each circumstance to recognize and accept that you have created the circumstances before you. Or, you can blame others, or the world, or God, and continue to be the victim that you apparently relish being. How easy it would be to take full responsibility for your life by changing your thoughts and actions, and have the power to change your circumstances and make them what you would prefer them to be instead.

We are here to help you at this time to make this transition easier—to help you understand the world better and how to live in it easier. You have struggled long enough. It is time to spell things out for you, so that you fully comprehend and understand the parameters within which to operate and excel in your life. Life can get easier and easier by following the dictates the Source has put forth for your understanding, growth, and development. By following these dictates, you have the opportunity to excel, not only personally, but professionally, and economically as well.

The time has come for people, all mankind, to operate from right thinking, right action, and right being. We are here to help you, one and all. All the heavens are here to support you in this endeavor. Your life is at stake at this time. You can adhere to the dictates of the Source, your God, or perish in the process. No man will be left behind if he does not adhere to these dictates. It has been given. It is now written.

CHAPTER ONE

You Matter: Following Your Calling

The struggles of man put aside, the planet and its people are moving forward at light speed. Mankind has taken hold of the idea of spirituality first and foremost and has begun to embrace the fact that it is the way of the future. Man's way of manipulation has not worked. It may supply a temporary fix; but only temporary, as there are residual effects to manipulation. Many men do not see, but it is felt throughout mankind and eternity. You do not realize the impact your thoughts, acts, or deeds have upon one another and the rest of humanity. You struggle and in your efforts to avoid struggle, you put a bandage on a situation only to find out that the bandage did not stick. *Nothing sticks like Divinity.* Man's idea of quick fixes only prolongs the agony. It also delays his development and contribution to the world. We are all here to make a contribution. No one gets away with not contributing. However, the choices we make dictate the contribution we end up making. If you make the contribution you were sent to make, you make a positive impact on society at large. If you shirk your responsibility, you also have a ripple effect on mankind and diminish what could have been. If everyone did as they were told, all would be well and in balance.

But man has his own idea of how it should be. He wants it his way. Well, how is that working? It's not in most cases, because man is delivering his message in a guarded, slanted and altered view. He is living his life out of fear-based decisions and affecting mankind in a negative rather than positive way.

If man took responsibility for who he is, how he is living, and what he is contributing, he would think differently as he would realize that who he is matters. And, he matters not only to his immediate family and environment, but also to the world at large. All on the planet have a contributing force to contend with, and they make a choice on a daily basis as to how they contribute. Are you contributing in a positive or a negative manner?

You think you're the only one who knows you, but that is not true. We all know. Each and every individual in existence knows who you are and what you do and how you live. You can't hide. Some of you believe you can actually hide from God; that God doesn't notice. He notices everything! Believe me. He doesn't miss a trick. You think you are getting away with something and you're not. Not in the least. You can't hide a thing. You can't hide anything on the global level either. We are all one in the universe coming out of the same Source, believe it or not. The ramification of that is that on some level, we all know one another and are responsible for one another. If you recognize that one fact, you will begin treating each other with more respect and tolerance. Your brethren are only a reflection of and a different aspect of you. You cannot hide who you are from them no more than they can hide themselves from you.

Each individual may not be consciously aware enough to recognize and fully comprehend this fact; however, knowing this as truth may cause you to live your life a bit differently. Could you imagine a world wherein all treated each other well, knowing that the way they treat others was only a reflection of how they treat themselves? If you treat someone badly, you are only demonstrating to him or her how badly you think of and treat yourself.

You can't hide from anyone anymore. Too many people on the planet are becoming "conscious," aware, so those who remain "unconscious" and who operate in that manner will stand out in the crowd, and not necessarily in a positive way. Do you want attention drawn to you because of your lack of true worldliness, because of your inability to know who you are both as an individual and in context with the world in which you live?

People often chuckle about or ridicule those they do not understand—psychics, people who see ghosts and spirits, who believe in reincarnation or even those who believe in God, for that matter (or are vocal about it). People who laugh and carry on, and criticize those who have an insight of more than meets the eye, are only demonstrating their ignorance and lack of personal growth to the world. Just because they can't see something themselves, does not mean it doesn't exist. But, so many stand up and ridicule others so vocally it's laughable. The loudest think that they are the smartest. If they only knew how ridiculous they appeared to others who really know, they might quiet their stand in public. How embarrassing for people who tout this theory and that theory, knowing nothing of what they speak.

But those who do know usually remain quiet because they fear being ridiculed. They give their power to these louts because they are afraid of what people will say and think of them. What does it matter if it's the truth? Wouldn't you rather take a stand for what you know and believe, than cower to those who are ignorant because you value their opinion of you? The need for acceptance has held mankind back from full self-expression for eons because they are more worried about what people think of them than what job they are to do while living on this planet.

Think more about what you are to do for mankind than what mankind will think of you. The judgments they make are judgments more of themselves than of you. Let them judge you if that is to be, rather than deny yourself and the world of your divine purpose, and make that contribution. Be true to yourself and to your Source.

Believing in following the Source, a power higher than yourself, does not diminish you in any way. You are made of the same cloth. It is what it is. You cannot define it; nor can you separate from it. It is what it is. Why not accept it for what it is and embrace it and capitalize on it rather than fight and resist it? You are fighting with an ego that is afraid to be diminished in any manner. If you were to accept that you are one with the Source, how diminished could you be? You are one powerful individual in my book!

But you prefer ego-driven experiences; have the need to be separate in order to feel special. You are special by just being. You are an individual. Just because you are loved equally or are equally powerful does not make you less than another. You are each special in your own unique way.

Express that uniqueness by utilizing the gifts and talents you were given for the purpose you are to fulfill this lifetime.

I'm not saying each person's divine purpose is in any way indicative of having to make a spiritual contribution, be part of some movement, etc. If your divine purpose is to be a secretary, be one wholeheartedly. Choose it because you desire it and have a calling to be that, not because it's a way to make a living. It should be the job you choose because it's innate to you and your highest good. If your calling is to be a truck driver, be that happily. Embrace that role, enjoy it, and don't think you are less than someone else because others think you should be something else. If your divine purpose is to be a comedian, a singer or a lifeguard embrace those as well, knowing that you are serving a divine purpose by fulfilling that role. There are more than a few jobs to fill in the world. Not all divine purposes need be filled for income either. You may serve a divine purpose by being a certain way or doing certain activities, and you bring those qualities to specific work or play, through daily activities that allow you to express what you need to express to be fulfilled in this lifetime.

Do those activities joyfully. Do not resist what you have a calling to do. It is imperative that you follow your calling. You were meant to do something with your life. Figure it out or allow it to occur out of what is natural for you. What are you drawn to do? Do you feel a profound need to do something? Then that's something you need to do. Do it quickly and do it joyfully. Do not wait for permission or the right timing or anything else that you can potentially put in your path as a deterrent. The faster you step into your right role, the faster the world will be at peace and in balance. Are you willing to do your part?

What are you to be? What are you to do? Think about what drives you forward naturally. What would you do if you didn't have to worry about the income or what the neighbors thought? If the world was sitting in wait for you to pick anything in it that you could want or be, who would you be and what would you choose?

Now, look at that and determine all the reasons why you won't or think you can't do what you want. If there is a path you were meant to follow, follow it. If you won't, really look at why and remove those blocks whether they are internal or external. If you were meant to do something specific with your life, the life forces will support you in that endeavor. You will be amazed at how easy life is when you are doing what you were supposed to do. All of the universe will support any endeavor that is perfect and right for you.

The only reason that you don't know what your calling is, is fear-based and you are blocking the knowledge, understanding, and acceptance of it. Look at the fear. Why would you be afraid of expressing your true nature? Why are you unclear as to your true nature? What do you suppose are your thoughts that block you from accepting the ideas that come to you? If you get the sense that you would prefer doing X and then judge X, look at that and answer why you are judging it. What is your programming that says you shouldn't or couldn't do something?

It is your choice. It is your choice to listen to your higher calling or to your programming. And, where did this programming come from? Well-meaning family, friends, teachers, society, etc., have dictated their opinions and judgments and passed them down from others, who have been mutually accepted as authority figures of sorts. It is time to begin thinking for yourself and determine the beliefs appropriate for a particular situation.

The appropriate belief for you to fulfill your calling would be more in line with *I can do this. This should be easy for me. I love doing this. This brings me joy and satisfaction.*

At no time in history has there been a more serious time for you to get into your right role. It is imperative for each individual as well as mankind at large. All benefit from each being in their right place performing their right work. Now is the time to take stock of whether or not you are delivering your highest purpose to the world and mankind. Are you making a contribution by expressing who you are? Or, are you following a fear-based existence by doing what you think is necessary for money and approval?

It is your choice, but remember—the choices you make impact not only the quality of your life but also the quality of life of those around you, as well as life of the planet.

CHAPTER TWO

All Relationships: Issues of Fear and Control

You struggle with all relationships, and not just spousal or dating ones. All stress in relationships comes from within you, each and every one of you. Your tendency, however, is to blame the other person for what they are or are not doing. It has nothing to do with the problems you are having; that is your perception only.

What someone else does or doesn't do is irrelevant. You are the one with the issues when something disturbs you. However, you don't look at yourself. It's rare if you do. Take a look now at how you are operating in your relationships. Are they smooth? Effortless? Easy? Loving? Joyful? If not, look at yourself and find within what is disturbing you and fix that; don't look outside of yourself.

Most people focus on being a victim of another person and their behavior. The other person is only acting out behavior that you attract. If another does something that doesn't bother you, then there is no issue. If they do something that does bother you, look at yourself and yourself only. Once you clear up what's within you, one of two things will happen—you will not be bothered by that behavior any more or that person won't do what bothers you.

You need to look at yourself and yourself only because you hold the key to all behavior, both bad and good. The behavior permeates throughout humanity and shows up in your life for you to experience, and what goes on within you also shows up worldwide. All of humanity and the stresses in the world lie within you to handle and all you need to do is work on yourself in order to affect the rest of the world. If you want peace in the world, focus on creating peace within yourself. If you want peace in your household, work on peace within yourself. They are only a reflection of you.

Instead, you will blame your children, your spouse, or your in-laws for the experiences you have rather than take a deep, hard look at yourself. It is both simple and not so simple. It is much simpler to look at yourself and change *you* than to try and get someone else to change. It is also *difficult* to look at yourself, especially when you must go deep inside and look at things that are unpleasant to you. There are those who spew anger and resentment at those around them wasting precious time that could be applied to searching for the answers within. The answers lie there and are accessible if you just take the time to look.

Remember who you are and the Divinity within. The Divinity within has all the answers. If you let go and let God help you discover the answers, He will reveal them to you if you cannot come up with them on your own.

Take a look at *all* your relationships. What do they teach and show you? How do they make you feel? Look at your reaction. What does it tell you? What do you need to hear? You have only to look as close as your own thoughts for the answers you seek. Don't delude yourself thinking that the cause of your relationship problems lies outside of you because it does not. Man is running around trying to find perfect relationships or change one into a perfect relationship. It cannot happen. All someone can do is work on themselves and bring themselves into balance, peace, and harmony in order to have that reflected in their outer experience.

Each relationship is designed as a mirror. Your relationship to money, things, behavior, people, activities, etc, is all a reflection of your thoughts about yourself and the world. As you relate to one thing, you relate to another. Focus on one relationship and all others will be impacted. Focus on improvement of any aspect of your life and all others will improve as well.

Cleanse your soul of the burdens of behaviors and beliefs that diminish who you are and the relationships you have, whether those relationships are with people or inanimate objects. Look at yourself and yourself alone to see what your relationship is to yourself. The way you relate to yourself is how others relate to and treat you. How others react to you is a reflection of what you believe about yourself. You have only to look outside of yourself to what others are doing to you that bothers you to know what is going on within yourself. It is an easy litmus test, this mirror you have ready and available on a daily basis. There is no escaping it, as there is no escaping you.

If you are having a problem, the problem lies within you. If you are not having a problem, it's because there is no problem within you. When you have a problem, look at yourself and yourself alone. The symptom that shows up as a problem is your opportunity to recognize that something is out of balance within yourself that needs to be corrected. Once you look at yourself, you determine the right action moving forward. Correct your thinking first; the right action will unfold naturally. It always does.

You spend much too much time focusing on why you have become a victim rather than on what is within you that is contributing to this circumstance. If only you would look at yourself, there would be many less problems. Not only would you uncover the solution much quicker, but by also eliminating blame, wars would not exist. There would be no need, because everyone would recognize that the cause of the problem lies only within themselves.

Each and every one of you has the ability to stop wars by releasing the cause or need to fight from within yourself. Why do you think fighting back or fighting for a cause is the solution? If you eliminate the belief from within yourself, you will eliminate the need to fight *anyone at any time.*

You need to stay home more and look at yourself. You run off to war to fight for a cause. You run around your neighborhood looking for solutions to the problems at hand. Why not stay home and figure it out on your own? Why bother others with your problems and concerns? Why not leave them alone to determine the solutions to the dilemmas that have been caused? If everyone stopped discussing and started processing their woes, the world would be a much happier place.

When you have a problem, you pick up the phone and call your friend or counselor. Why? Because you don't know who you are. You don't realize that you caused the problem and that you have the solution already within you. Rather than take the time to sit down and evaluate your thought process, you run to another individual seeking answers and solace outside of yourself. Some are so attached to the idea of drama that the thought of *really* finding a solution is frightening.

You enjoy struggle, drama, and upset and complain continuously when life could be so easy and effortless for you all. You wonder how you got into this pickle or that. Why me? You cry, you scream, you pray, you complain, so on and so forth. But why, when you can have peace and balance in your life? Your life really should be without stress and drama. It is obvious to me that no one believes that because they seem to be committed to stress as part of their life but it really isn't necessary. You can let go of that whole concept if you choose. What do you choose?

The life you are living is the life you chose. If you decide it is not the right fit any longer, you can choose again and choose what is more appropriate. All change can actually be effortless as well. Your labels are what keep you bound to old and outmoded thinking which, in turn, keeps you playing and performing old programming about how life should be according to, most likely, people who are now dead.

How many of you realize that you are living your life based on what people did centuries and eons ago, and you are living by automatic pilot rather than thinking for yourself? Who said life had to be the way you perceive it to be? Was it your mother, or her mother, or her mother's mother? Or a teacher, explorer, or scientist somewhere? Who are you listening to? Who set the rules that you follow day in and day out, lifetime after lifetime? Have you ever stopped to think that you are living someone else's life, their decisions, their visions, their fears, and limitations?

You are made up of thoughts and beliefs that have been passed on to you by society, parents, teachers, the media, the government, and anyone else who chose to express an opinion. Just because it's something that has the masses believing and/or doing does not mean it's right or correct for you. You have choice and free will.

I am not suggesting that upon reflection, if you don't perceive a law to be necessary for a current circumstance, you take it upon yourself to break it. You could take it upon yourself, however, to recognize its applicability today and change it. However, if everyone were tuning in, the laws may not be necessary. Take the red traffic light for example. I'm not saying that because the law says you shouldn't run a red light, you should decide to do it because you think you should. But if everyone were tuning in, looking at themselves and themselves alone and following their Divine guidance, the need for the red light would not exist. In that state of living your truth with Divine guidance, all mankind would be in their right place at the right time and no one would be colliding with anyone else. Hence, no need for the red light to control traffic.

The need to control is a fear-based expression. Once people have eliminated their fears, they would no longer have the need to control others. When people stop trying to control one another, everyone would relax. Fear complicates everything. By learning to let go of fear, everyone would relate to the world as it truly should be. Fear permeates throughout mankind and wreaks havoc even where people don't have a clue it's touching or affecting them.

Fear can be eliminated from the planet if people could only eliminate it from within themselves. If there is any fear on the planet, it lies within you somewhere. Where you need to look is within and uncover every possible morsel before looking to see it disappearing elsewhere. You have carried fear for so long, it feels right and comfortable. It's the rare individual who knows no fear. People can eliminate fear within themselves, making life seem easy for them and helping them move in the direction of Divine guidance in an effortless way. Without fear, there is nothing stopping you from expressing to the world who you are and who you were meant to be.

Each and every day that you can eliminate fear, it is further eliminated from mass consciousness. The more fear that is eliminated, the less fear there is overall. That could be a major contribution to the planet. By looking at yourself and your own fears, you can eliminate stress and struggle for people around the world. You are all connected, so your impact is felt in more ways than one. Not only in the way that you relate to your immediate surroundings and those around you, but also the elimination of fear within you can impact those across the globe that you have met or even those you may never meet.

Your work on yourself can be profound at best. If you choose not to work on yourself, you can leave people devastated and struggling for eons to come. What a gift you can give the world by just working on your own fears, limiting beliefs, and cowardice.

CHAPTER THREE

Preparing For Heaven On Earth

At no other time in history have so many elements come together toward a certain end as beautifully as the coming of this new millennium. At this time, there are so many synergies blending together toward the same end or goal to enter into the new millennium. The current time in history is so magical and so important that no one realizes its full impact or significance. This new millennium is what everyone has been waiting for, but rather than relish this newness and excitement of what is coming or occurring, everyone is wrapped up in their own "stuff"—anguish of eons that is surfacing right now to be cleansed in preparation of the new millennium.

Everyone is panicking over the chaos of their own life and not realizing they are on the last legs of cleansing eons of time that came before, which is contributing to their suffering now. They are purging that which doesn't work. It is all coming up fast and furious. No one seems to be able to get a handle on it. The time has come for all mankind to awaken to the truth. No one really understands what is going on. People feel and act as if the world is coming to an end, when the very opposite is true. We are just on the cusp of a very new beginning. The new beginning of heaven on earth as has been predicted for eons of time.

The time has come to rejoice in the magnificence of this time here on earth. At no time in history has so much culminated to one end—the end of the separation between heaven and earth. In its coming together, all mankind will be set free. Those who remain here will float, as if living a whole new existence without struggle and strife. Those who are not adapting to the new lifestyle will move on when and where it is appropriate. No one needs to worry. What they need to do is pay attention.

Start paying attention to the world around you. How are you reacting to it? What are you doing about it? How are you participating in it? Think about the dynamics of your own personal situation. Keep in mind that everyone is in the same boat, experiencing the same or similar experiences and emotions as you. What you do about them will dictate the results you get. Experience the moment for what it is and learn from it. It is not shaping your destiny as much as your viewpoint is.

Take heed. The time has come for *all* to be brought back into balance. Do this now. Take heed of your current circumstances. Are you living your life's desire? Are you doing the right thing for yourself and others? Are you doing the best you can in any given situation? Think about how you are being and what you are doing in the world. Are you doing what is naturally true for you, right and perfect according to God? Or your parents? Or society? Or are you acting out of need for money? Out of greed? Out of lack? What is the basis for your choices? Do you make them consciously or unconsciously? The time has come for you to take stock of your life and everyone in it. Are they meant to be by your side, or have the relationships around you withered and you are hanging on out of security or obligation? No relationship should be endured for the wrong reasons. The right reason is they are meant to intermingle with your path in life. There is a reason higher than you know for your personal interactions with others.

Take stock now of the relationships you share and make sure they are divinely right for you. Do not have *any* relationship out of obligation as it will both throw you off balance and have long-term detrimental effects. *Do not*, I say, *do not* stay in a relationship with anyone you are not to be in a relationship with for any reason. Doing so will become toxic to you both.

Take heed of your life and this warning. You are meant to be a divine being associated with divine beings. All those who are not treating you divinely should be eliminated from your life. You only need do this by making a choice to associate with those who uplift you. If you feel the need to explain yourself to those you have chosen not to include in your life because of their negativity, tell them how you feel. Make it clear to those individuals that you no longer want to be held back by negative actions or thinking. If they want to remain friends, they must change their ways and uplift themselves. Do not maintain toxic relationships of any sort. It is imperative that you let go of all relationships not mutually supportive and appropriate.

CHAPTER FOUR

Overcoming Financial Struggle

People struggle with their finances day in and day out, not realizing they are the cause of the lack in their lives. They look at the economy as the cause. They look at their parents. They look at their jobs. They look at their businesses. But at no time are they looking at themselves. Their finances are in direct proportion to how they look at themselves. Their finances reflect what they think of themselves; how they relate to the world at large. What kind of life they desire. What they believe they can have and not have. What people receive has nothing to do with what they do. They do whatever relates to how they feel about themselves and what they feel they would be able to receive or accept.

They have what they believe they can handle. They demonstrate to the world what they believe about themselves, who they believe they are, and what they believe they deserve. If they want more money, the first place to look is within to discover what is making them tick. What causes them to believe what they believe? Where did those thoughts come from that dictate their life and lifestyle? That is where they should concentrate their energy. In the thoughts that created the thoughts that dictate the results within which they live.

Where people usually "live" is in the victim role of "there's not enough." It seems to them that there is not enough because of their belief that there is not enough. For many, there is abundance and surplus. For the majority, there is not enough—that group consciousness needs to acquire the same group consciousness of those who live in abundance. To live in abundance is not magical or beyond people's ability. It is magical only in that the thoughts that permeate throughout the minds of those who "do not have" are imbedded in their roots and are difficult to access. Those thought patterns have lived so long within their ancestry and in their programming that it is sometimes difficult for them to fathom that their reality is only their reality due to their own programming.

What I find fascinating is how often money can become a pure obsession. Everyone operates so profoundly around its base and yet it is only a reflection of the mind itself and a useful tool in society. Money is not meant to rule an existence, which it does for many. It has become a god to many because they can't see beyond its existence and need. The need has become so profound that people obsess over it and run their lives around it. Again, it is a tool. A useful tool, but a tool nonetheless.

I find it difficult to get through to those who desire money—that they do not need to go out and try to make more money as much as they need to sit back and determine the line of thinking that is running their life and to change it. If they change their thinking, they can change their reality of money. Income streams exist for all. No one is left out of this dynamic. There are only more for some based on their choices and decisions. But those choices and decisions are based on the thoughts behind them. It is not the other way around.

If someone wants to change their financial circumstances, they need to change how they look at money. How they view money is how their money will appear to them. If they change their view of money, their reality of money will change. There is no scarcity of money in the world. No one needs to go without. No one is meant to suffer and no one needs to continue to do so unless they choose to do so.

You can choose in any given moment to change your financial picture by changing your financial mind. It's the financial mind within that dictates the results without. Change the mind; change the money. Where do you start? Start at the beginning. Start by thinking of all the thoughts you have ever had about money. Write them down. Write an exhaustive list of all thoughts about money. Once you are done, put down next to each and every thought the source who told you that was so. Who taught you that particular "fact" about money?

What were their circumstances? How did they live? Are they people you would like to emulate? If you are taking financial advice from people who do not have money, it is time to listen to people who do have money. Find people who you can speak to and learn from or read about that have money. What do they believe and say about money? Decide who you would like to listen to. Who has the results that you would like to duplicate? If they have the type of reality and results you prefer, then by all means follow them.

The other is to determine your possibility by asking Divinity directly. Ask Him how much money you are entitled to receive. Ask how you are best to acquire it. Ask the line of work best suited to you. You may not have an issue with money as much as you may have made a wrong choice in the line of work you chose. If you were in the right line of work, you may find making money becomes much easier.

Those who are in the wrong line of work are creating an imbalance for themselves and others, and money isn't attracted to imbalanced situations. When your situation is balanced and you are in your right job, it is much easier for money to come to you because its right channels and circumstances exist.

Most people are working in jobs they hate because they don't feel they can make money at what they love to do. It is, again, not about the money. It is about the way you view money. All of you who are in the wrong job could do more for yourselves, your families, and the world by getting into your right job immediately. If everyone gave up having to work for a living and did what they were supposed to, no one would be working for money and they would have the money they deserved.

The right people in the right jobs would be making the right money and no one would be just surviving any longer. They would have been moved into a life of abundance because they are living an abundant life. Doing one's right work is living in abundance and is also contributing to an abundant life.

What people hold onto is their fears, their anxieties and their beliefs. They often do not believe they could make a living doing what they desire. If they did what they desired, all would be happier, including the planet as a whole.

It is time for people to move into their right place, their right jobs, and do the work they chose to do before coming to this planet. Everyone came with a mission and a particular skill set to achieve that mission. Most are not even close to fulfilling that mission because they are off running here and there trying to make a buck. If they gave up that search, they could be in the right livelihood making the right living, and contributing to the planet as they were meant to contribute.

Not all gifts are meant to be given to the world at a price. Many people are here without the need to make a living or to have a job. They may still have valuable work to contribute by demonstrating the gifts and talents they possess, but they don't need to be paid for them. Some will find circumstances that support them being who they are without the need to work for money. Others will give their gifts so naturally that whatever they do they will be expressing those gifts, without money being an issue.

The point is that everyone, and I mean everyone, needs to be expressing his or her divine purpose here while on this planet. No one has ever been granted special dispensation from expressing his or her divine purpose. Everyone has a role to perform. It is your choice as to whether or not you perform it and how well you perform it.

Are you willing to take on your chosen role and live it to the fullest? Become the best at that role? Or, are you just going to haphazardly demonstrate your skills and talents to the world? Trying to get by without contributing your best, causes imbalance for yourself and others. No one benefits from your laziness, your fears, or your lack of vision and everyone benefits from your commitment to your own life and living your vision and mission. People thrive when they are on purpose and those around them reap numerous benefits because of it.

It is time for all to take their right role—take a stand at being the individual they came to be and live the life they were meant to live. If by chance, a person came to learn something from a life of struggle or lack, it doesn't mean that they have to live in that world or state for long. The sooner they learn the lesson, the sooner they can achieve abundance throughout all areas of their life. They may need to learn humbleness by being poor. That doesn't mean they have to remain poor the rest of their life. There is no honor in being poor. It does provide a viewpoint, however, that may impact how a person views the world and treats others. It may offer them compassion for the plight of others. It doesn't mean they have to remain there to be loyal to anyone who chooses to remain there. Being loyal to people who are poor by remaining one of them does them no honor or help. All it does is reinforce to them that there is no choice and allows them to be complacent by remaining there.

It is sometimes easier and more comfortable for some to wallow in their mishaps and problems than to take responsibility for their circumstances. Everyone deserves abundance. But to have abundance one may have to do something about it. Like change their thinking. Sounds easy to some; to others it's the most difficult thing they will ever do in their lives. Changing one's belief system and one's way of thinking that has become so imbedded may be the hardest thing one will ever do with their life. But unless they learn to be able to change their mind, they will be a victim of the thoughts and ideas of others forever. That serves no one.

What works for one at one time, may not work for everyone all the time. It is time people thought for themselves. It is time they stopped and realized how they are living and why. Who chose the life they are living? Them, their parents, a schoolteacher, a spouse, a friend, or society? What is in it for them to remain in that position? What would be possible if they chose the life they were meant to have? By performing one's right work, all possibilities open up far beyond anyone's comprehension because they are limited in their thinking about reality. The reality for many, if not most, is *this is the way it is.* There is no more *limiting* thought than that.

This is only the way you think it is. It can be any way you want it to be. It doesn't have to look like anything it has been, anything you have been told, or anything you can imagine. It can be something totally different. It can be beyond your wildest dreams. The problem is that you will never know it if you do not change your thinking about your life, your abilities, and your possibilities. Only you can make that difference. Only you can take a stand to have the life you desire and make the choices necessary to support that decision.

Whatever is to come is out of your belief system. If you do not change your belief system, you will not change anything else around you. Whatever you have now will be what you will have down the road, unless you change your beliefs about it.

The time has come for everyone to take responsibility for the lives they have chosen and continue to choose to live. If you wish to be living in abundance, get into your right livelihood; start living your passions, experience life to the fullest. Give up pleasing some memory that no longer serves you. Choose another life and lifestyle. It is all possible for you.

At no time in history has it been so important for man to step into their right roles. All need to be brought into balance. All need to be in their right roles in order for the planet to be balanced properly. If you are doing a job that is meant for someone else, give it up so they can have it. Do not deny them their right place because of your fear. Let go and let God help you put yourself into your right place making the living appropriate to you, which, by the way, still does not necessarily have anything to do with abundance in the pocketbook. It is only a portion of what is available to you. God is your Source for *all* abundance. The employer is not the only source. It is an avenue of income. It is not the only one unless you choose to believe it is. God is your Source, and is an infinite one. You need not limit your job possibilities by the income attached to it.

CHAPTER FIVE

Listening To That Small Voice Within

This age; this time in history has been a long time in coming. All roads have led to this time and place. A new beginning. This is a new beginning for us all. The time has come for repentance, forgiveness, and a new beginning. No longer can people continue as they have running this way and that, not knowing their purpose, not doing their rightful jobs, not living the life they were meant to live. The time has come for people to return to balance in all aspects of their lives and be with the people they should be with, do the jobs they have longed to do, and express their divinity within, without, and throughout all aspects of their lives.

Since the beginning of time, there have never have so many situations that have occurred in sequence toward an end result such as now. There are many things going on in the world today that have been predestined and expected, as well as more and different experiences than were anticipated because of the advancement of mankind. You are better off than anticipated. You have grown better and stronger than expected. You have done more for the planet than expected. It is time for you to be rewarded for all that you have endured, created, rebalanced, and corrected.

Those of you who have looked within, taken responsibility for yourselves, and have done the right thing for all concerned, will be rewarded beyond your wildest dreams. Those who have not taken responsibility, will not be rewarded and will be made to pay for their mistakes now at this time. It is not an easy task punishing and rewarding those in kind. We wish for all to be treated well.

We want everyone to win and succeed. But too often the messages from God have been given and have fallen on deaf ears. The unwillingness to hear and adhere to the will of God has cost everyone dearly. Those of you who continue not to listen, will be punished. But not punished in a way you would probably anticipate. You will be punished by being denied heaven on earth. Heaven on earth will be for those who embrace it because they have embraced God and followed His word. No, you do not have to be perfect. You already are. Yes, you will continue to make mistakes and fall back into human behavior; that is not the point. The point is what is within your own heart. How do you live and express your desires and who you are?

Are you true to yourself and your God almighty? Or, are you selfish and think of yourself and yourself alone? Do you live a balanced and fruitful life? Or, are you depriving yourself and others of what God has given and dictated?

Do you wish to go it alone? Do you wish to remain separated from the Source? Your Source? The Source of all your good and the good of others? So many of you run around looking for answers outside of yourself, trying to make a quick buck; trying to put a bandage on a situation. The quick fix, however, doesn't work. It never has and never will. What you need is what lies within you at your core. That is what will make you happy. That is what will make you wealthy. That is what will bring the love you desire, and deserve, into your life. It is not outside of yourself anywhere. No one has the answers that do not already lie within.

So, stop running around, looking and listening to others. Start listening to yourself and the small voice inside of you that has been trying to be heard for eons of time. The small voice that has so much power it can save your life and the world at large. That small voice that lies so quietly within is urging to come out and be heard, to be listened to, and adhered to. That small voice is what will save your life and your meager existence. That is what you need to listen to. The answers are not found on TV, in the news, or from the minister, teacher, or the government. No one but that small voice within you must be listened to and adhered to. When you begin to do that, you will begin to see your life change, and change in dramatic ways.

The day you trust yourself and that small voice within, will be the day your life will change for the better. Listen to those outside of you, and your life will continue to diminish, be harried, be frustrated, be torn, be stressed, so on and so forth. You have come to a pivotal place in humanity and its growth. This time in history is like no other because you are given a choice. A choice to adhere to the word of God, or to perish from this planet. You can choose to live here as heaven comes to earth or you can choose to move on to another environment. This may not be the place for you to live. It is time for those who are rightfully inheriting the kingdom of God to remain as heaven is brought down to them, or leave to a more suitable environment for their thinking. It is your choice; always your choice.

The time has come for man to stop blaming those around him for their troubles. Their troubles are not caused by those around them. Not listening to and following that small voice within them is the cause of their troubles. Their lack of trust in themselves and their higher power is diminishing their lives and existence substantially. Those who listen to the word of God and that small voice within will excel at everything. As they begin to trust themselves without a shadow of a doubt, they will begin to soar and express a glorious life. They will be amazed and saddened by the fact that it took so long for them to have the life they desired, knowing they could have had it all along, but willingly denied themselves by their lack of willingness to listen to that small voice within.

At no time in history will mankind so rejoice as to the excellence of their existence and how easy life can be once they begin to listen to the small voice within. The small voice within will become louder and louder as mankind begins to listen more and more and follow its dictates more consistently. You will see profound change around you as people begin to listen to that voice and follow its instruction. More and more people will listen, adhere, and be in their right place for their higher good. What will happen? People will become happy again. They will rejoice in the ease and effortlessness of their lives and wonder why they didn't think to do this a long time ago and avoid all the self-inflicted trauma on themselves by looking outside of themselves. They will know that all this time they could have been listening to themselves, and that small voice within, and had a totally different experience in their lives.

What sadness will abound when they realize they could have changed their lives so profoundly a long time ago but chose not to listen. That realization will cause sadness. But let it go, as the time has come for all mankind to rejoice in this profound news and the ability to once again be true to themselves by listening to the voice within—the voice that will save their lives. The voice that will guide them and protect them. The voice that has all the answers. The voice that will lead them in the right direction. The voice that will never let them down.

That small voice within will get louder and louder as time goes on, as the trust in that voice builds. You will one day be so in tune with that voice that you will no longer doubt it, or question following it. To that end, we will all rejoice. All the heavens will sing and applaud as you become confident in that small voice within.

CHAPTER SIX

You Make a Difference

The cries of mankind feel as if they have gone unheard. They have not. Believe me. They have not. We hear them loud and clear. We hear them day in and day out. But the cries go on and the answers abound. People are so attached to the cries that they are not listening to the answers that come. They seek the answers and yet they do not listen. They do not hear what we have to say. When we try to answer, they are usually too busy crying to hear what we are trying to say to them in order to help.

We are whispers in your ears. We are the sounds of the wind trying to inspire you to right action. We are always speaking to you but you are rarely listening. You want us to help; but you rarely listen to the help we are giving. What should we do? We continue to reach out to you, waiting and hoping that one day you will listen. We hope you will listen because we are more than happy to help you in whatever need that arises.

We do not sit in judgment of you. We do not sit back watching you struggle without trying to assist. We are there to help you every step of the way. But you ask without believing we can or would help you. You struggle assuming that is the way of the future and that is just the way it is. You ask for help not believing it will really come your way or that you deserve the outcome you desire.

What is that all about? Well, please allow me to answer that struggle permeates throughout mankind. You don't think you are worthy of our help or the results we can give. You feel guilty for turning your back to God over and over again. You do this unconsciously, of course, but when you determine you need His help, you do not feel worthy of receiving it because you have turned your back so often. You do not feel you have the right to ask for and receive the help.

You don't feel worthy, as you feel completely undeserving of God's help because you have turned your back on Him so often. You have chosen money over God. You have chosen man over God. You have chosen your own greed over God. Over and over again you have chosen not to listen to the word of God. Since you ignore Him and unconsciously are aware of the fact that you ignore Him, you do not feel deserving of His forgiveness and willingness to give to you unconditionally.

You may have been forgiven countless times, but you have not forgiven yourself. You hold yourself accountable for everything that goes wrong, although you won't admit it. You feel so guilty about so many things, it is too long a list to count. You would be surprised how hard you all are on yourselves. God is much kinder to you than you ever have been or possibly could be.

What has become of man is that he bears the guilt of lifetimes and of his forebears. He carries the guilt of long-deceased family members who sit on the other side wishing they could help, as the sins of the father certainly do pass onto their descendants. At no time before in history has this been so prevalent. The reason is that this is the first time in history that these past mistakes can be washed cleaned so profoundly through one's own effort that all mankind can have a fresh start.

The problem is, however, that not enough of you can forgive yourselves. You would rather hold the memory of a past deed alive than to let it go and move on. You cling to the past so profoundly that you hold all of mankind back in the process. It is a shame to one extent that you are all interrelated as you end up holding each other back by keeping your garbage alive so intently.

On the other hand, one individual, by changing his beliefs and behavior, can profoundly impact all mankind to the same degree. All are one and one are all. No one escapes this dynamic. No one. If you think you are different, you are not. If you think you can get away with anything, you cannot. You cannot do much without the whole universe knowing or being affected by it.

It has come to pass that each one of you must become responsible not only for yourself but for everyone around you. This is not to say that each one of you must take on the roles and responsibilities of another but you must recognize that you are responsible for every individual in existence. Doing so, you must first become extremely conscious of the actions you take and the impact it has on those around you. You are responsible for the results and experiences of others. Therefore, when you are taking right action, they will reap the benefits. When you take actions that are inappropriate, they too will suffer the consequences of your ineffectiveness.

Do the right thing, and all will excel. Do the wrong thing and all will suffer. Of course, the ramifications will depend on the situation. The point is, your actions are not isolated and independent. Everything you do affects the universe at large. You would be surprised at the impact you have on the world.

I am not saying this to frighten you or to make you afraid of making the wrong move every step of the way. The point is, I want you to be clear that your actions make a difference one way or another. Consider the actions you take and make them consciously, so you are not doing things that negatively affect others by your unconscious awareness of this fact. Pay attention to how you live your life. Are you consciously aware of the effect you may have on others or are you just arbitrarily taking action regardless of its impact on others.

Chapter Seven

Vicious Cycle: Striving for Satisfaction

People struggle, worry, struggle, worry, and struggle day in and day out. It is a vicious cycle that everyone wants to, and should, get off. It is ineffective and not productive. It can be stopped and it is much easier than anyone realizes. It is incredibly easy when you think about it and just ask us for help. There is no reason for everyone to continue at the pace that they operate currently at on this planet.

They are continually striving for something that does not exist. They are looking outside of themselves for a quality of life that only comes from within. They search for answers, truths, and solutions that only come with a true connection to God, their Source, the almighty.

So often people are running this way and that trying to accomplish one thing or another and what they are searching for is the satisfaction that comes from being one with their Creator. When they are one with their Creator, they need not search for this experience and that experience because once they are connected to the Source, their Creator, they are one with a stream of experience particular to them and their blueprint and purpose. They need not run around searching for something that lies within.

Unfortunately, they do not realize what they are really looking for or are missing. They only know that something is missing and they think that by going for this job, that experience, or try a particular activity, etc, that the solution will magically appear and they will have found that which they have searched for eons of time. But because it is not found outside of themselves and that is where they are searching, they keep looking in the wrong places and, therefore, always come up empty. No one will find the satisfaction in the outside world that comes from being connected to their Source, their God.

Once connected to that infinite supply and Source, all things are added. Everything that is right and appropriate for that individual is in their lap in the most effortless manner they could have ever imagined. They do not have to look for it, as what they were looking for will find them. They need not reach for the stars as the stars will come to them.

CHAPTER EIGHT

Show The World Who You Are

What people search for is themselves and an acknowledgment of who they are. Because they do not know who they are, they look outside of themselves comparing themselves to those around them hoping to validate that they are acceptable.

What they do not realize is that all are one and no one out there is really separate from others. So while they try to validate themselves against another, they are only mirroring back who they really are. If people really understood who they really were, they would not need to look outside themselves. If they looked within, they would see how glorious they really are.

No one is really separate from another unless they chose to separate themselves. But all in the world is a reflection of some aspect of them and they cannot hide from that, no matter how much they try.

When one man judges another, he only judges himself. He is acknowledging to all that he sees something within himself that he finds distasteful. But rather than accept the flaw within, he judges another as if the flaw lies outside himself. If he recognized the flaw within, he would be able to change it. But by looking outside of himself, he only draws more attention to his flaw and the flaw remains as is because he does not recognize that it is within himself as well.

The trouble is, people continue to look outside of themselves blaming each other and circumstances around them rather than recognize and accept the cause and the solution both lie within. If he realized this point alone, he would realize how powerful he really was. But no man sees the power within; they usually see themselves as a victim of a world gone bad. The world has not gone bad; man just perceives it as so.

The world is fine. The world is getting better because man is getting better. And, by getting better, I mean, more and more are becoming attuned to who they are and taking responsibility for themselves and the world at large. The more people begin to take that role of responsibility, the quicker the world will become a better place to live. It is moving in that direction but rather slowly at best. People need to own this information and act upon it quickly if they want their world to change. I don't only mean the world at large either. I mean the world around them. Their home and their neighborhood are all a reflection of who they are and believe themselves to be.

The time has come for everyone to stand up and be counted and make a difference in the world by taking responsibility for it and their own circumstances within it. They are not isolated from the world, they are not victims of the world. They are responsible for the world. The world is not responsible for them. They are responsible for the world. The experiences people have in the world are in direct relation to the beliefs they have about the world and them in it.

Once they recognize and accept this fact, they can make new choices to relate to the world differently. Do you feel you are a victim? Well then, the time to change that belief is necessary in order to no longer be a victim. If you change that belief alone, you will have a substantially different outcome in your world immediately. There is no time like the present to give up being a victim to become a volunteer. And by volunteer, I mean volunteer what you want the world to reflect of you. Volunteer the choices of righteousness not victimhood. Be an example of strength, the pillar in the community. Be someone who will set the example of what is right and good. Do not judge others who are different or who follow a different path. Be the example rather than the victim.

Do not wallow in self-pity, as many of you do in one form or another. Be at one with the Source and demonstrate to the world who you can be, not what you have become.

CHAPTER NINE

Great Expectations

The thing people struggle with the most is issues about themselves. They are very hard on themselves in general. They expect more of themselves than they do of others. Although they often expect too much of others as well. The expectations are what get them into trouble. If they didn't have expectations, they wouldn't be disappointed. However, that is not to say you should not want something or expect to get it. People have expectations about how life should be, what someone should do or not do and then frequently they are disappointed. It is not that the other person is bad or wrong. It is only that they did not meet their expectations. It is their expectations that get people into trouble, not the other person disappointing them.

When you set out to believe that something should be a certain way and it isn't, you become disappointed. The problem lies in blaming the outside situation or person for not living up to your expectations. They did nothing more than be who and what they are. The disappointment comes out of your own expectations. No one or nothing else was the disappointment. However, so often you go into situations with expectations and then blame the other person or the situation for not meeting them. They are not to blame for not meeting your expectations. Your expectations were to blame. The false accusation then gets you into further trouble as it promotes ill will where none should exist.

If you have an agreement with someone as to how something should transpire, that is another matter. That agreement is set for expectations based on the reality of the discussion, determination, and agreement. The outcome should be what you expect based on the agreement set forth. However, most situations do not have an agreement. What someone brings to the table usually are unrealistic expectations because they do not have facts to base them on or they are basing their expectations on past experience. Neither is correct.

People spend a lot of time in disappointment because they have set forth expectations that are unrealistic. They quite often then translate that disappointment into a judgment of the individuals involved. You would be surprised at how insidious this is and how much it permeates throughout all humanity. No one is completely free of this scenario.

CHAPTER TEN

How the Angels Answer Your Prayers

Time and time again you struggle and pray while waiting for answers to your prayers. You think we will come in and magically make changes to your life. The majority of you block and sabotage the efforts we put forth. You ask, and we come to the rescue, so to speak. Sometimes you hear us; sometimes not. Sometimes you welcome us; sometimes not.

You lack such clarity in who we are and what we can do for you and how we can do it that you miss the opportunities before you for solutions to the problems you face. We are here for you every step of the way. We feel your pain but our hands are tied unless you ask for help and receive it when given. We give you help all the time. Countless times you ask; countless times we give; countless times you miss the signals and messages we bring. The solutions to your problems lie within. We try many ways at times to give you messages, trying to communicate in one form or another.

Sometimes it is funny to watch you struggle while we are standing right in front of you trying to direct you to the right solution and you neither hear nor see us. We whisper in your ear continuously telling you the right action to take but you do not hear us. Why? Because you think it is coming from you and you do not trust yourself. You doubt yourselves so much that you end up tuning out the solutions that are coming from above. Divine answers perfect and right for you in your current situation, and you completely miss them. The clues abound around you given to you in a variety of formats for you to get them. You would be amazed at how much effort we put into communicating with you and so few of you seem to get it. Since we don't tire in the effort, we continue, but it would make our lives and yours easier if you learned to listen and recognize the clues that abound.

First and foremost, if you stop running around looking for solutions outside yourself, it will be easier to hear the messages given to you. *You are so mired in the noise of life that you miss the whispers of wisdom that are all around and within you.* We use you as instruments to communicate our messages. If your friends, colleagues, and coworkers are telling you the same message, there may be something in the message that you need to hear. Oftentimes, we speak to you through others rather than directly to you. You will hear us if you learn to listen. You must learn to differentiate between your own thoughts and the thoughts that we are imbibing in you.

We speak to you directly all the time. It is the rare person who stops to listen. It is sometimes easier for us to speak to you through others because they are not as attached to the answer or the outcome as you may be at that time. They do not judge what they are receiving because they are not wallowing in their own thoughts about it. Of course, you need to be discerning with the advice received from others because not everyone is speaking the truth. Many are speaking from their egos, opinions, and judgments. But you will know when it is the truth if enough people are telling you the same thing. At least stop and pay attention to the message and consider what is being addressed.

We sometimes communicate the same messages in the same format or in a variety of ways in order to communicate the message so you will recognize it. If you hear something three times, it is usually a clear indication we are trying to tell you something. Listen. Pay attention to those signals. Anything repetitious has a message behind it. Not always is the message from us; sometimes it is a message you need to adhere to but often it is us trying to communicate our messages to you.

We are often struggling trying to get a message across to you and use a variety of means to deliver it. You may hear a song. You may hear a child cry at just the right moment. You may hear someone on the radio address a topic relevant to your needs. The TV may signal a direction you should take. We may whisper in your ear and back it up by other commentary from one individual or some form of media or another. Billboards, advertising, conversation, scenery, and animals all hold the answers and are used as forms of communication to get your attention and transmit the messages to you. The signals abound around you daily and you usually miss them because you aren't paying attention, you are not listening, and you are not recognizing that which is before you because you are so busy running this way and that putting out fires and preventing the next one.

If you stopped more frequently just to listen, it would be amazing what you would learn. It would also make your life much simpler. Wouldn't it be easier to know what to do than wonder and worry for days, making wrong decisions in the interim? You may make a decision that will not serve a higher purpose because you wouldn't take the time to sit and be with us and the help we offer you. What do you have to lose by trying it out for a change? Why not purposefully and intentionally sit down and speak to us and wait for an answer? Rather than pray, and cry, and carry on, and run around with meaningless chatter and purpose, actually pray and wait for the answer.

Although the answer does not always come in that instant, you may find that more answers come than not over time by the practice of sitting still and waiting for them. If you get in the habit of meditating on a daily basis, you will attune your mind and body to open up its receptors to the information that abounds around you. All answers are available to you at any given point if you only learn how to listen for them.

Do nothing and see what happens. It will be amazing for most of you who work day in and day out trying to make a buck, make ends meet, keep up with the Joneses, or any other old and outmoded idea you operate by on this planet. You waste your time on nothing but silliness half the time because most of the activities you perform have no real purpose. You would be surprised at how much time you could save if you only asked us what is right and purposeful for you and your blueprint.

I watch parents with their children, spending countless hours taking them to and from sporting events, cutting an enormous amount of time out of their day. Do you, as parents, realize that 90% of the sports you enroll your children in are not right for them? They are playing games to satisfy some ego-driven purpose within the parent rather than serve the ideal and perfect place that child needs to be to reach their full potential. Countless hours are wasted. Why? Because parents do not take the time to ask if it is the right activity for the child to participate in at that time. The time is significant because what is not right one day may be right the next and vice versa. As a parent, you need to ask for guidance when it comes to guiding your child's path.

You have been given an important responsibility in raising children. Take it to heart. You do not always have the answers, as you already know. However, the answers are as close as your fingertips. You need not wonder if you are doing the right thing. You can always just ask your higher power and us if you are doing the right thing. We know. We can tell in an instant whether something is right or wrong. We do not have to weigh everything like you do. You analyze things to death. You write things in one column or another, using statistics and mathematical equations to make a determination and all you need do is ask us and we will tell you.

It would certainly save you a lot of time and trouble. Could you imagine doing what was right and appropriate for you to do all the time? Could you imagine the impact that would have on your life, your family's life, and the world? How simple things would become if you just asked us what to do before doing it? Could you imagine how much easier it would be if you asked, followed our direction, ended up doing what was right and perfect, and eliminated a lot of the problems that occur because you spend your time in wrong activities or going in the wrong direction?

Wouldn't it be easier to ask us and do the right thing, than have to ask for our help to rectify a situation gone awry? Of course, we would have a lot less to do with our time if we did not have to continually bail you out of problems, problems that could have been avoided by taking right action in the first place.

It has come to a point in time where enough of you have stopped to listen to us that we are being heard by more and more of you. Those of you who try to listen to us intentionally will begin to hear our voices, both audibly and in whispers. You will begin to recognize us in your daily activities and see how we try to communicate with you regularly.

You will begin to recognize the signals we give and begin to trust and adhere to them.

And as you continue to strengthen your willingness to listen and trust, our messages will become stronger and stronger, and your lives will become simpler and simpler. To that end, we all pray.

CHAPTER ELEVEN

Learn From Your Mistakes

What has come before you countless times is the opportunity to rectify the decisions and mistakes you have made in the past. Opportunities to learn lessons abound and you take in the lessons each and every time you make a mistake. Sometimes you learn significantly enough to not repeat the mistake, other times you do not. You have an opportunity today to begin a new approach in your life by not making the mistakes in the first place. You no longer need to keep doing the wrong things over and over to get the message.

You can now ask us for right and perfect action for you to take at this time. Should you choose not to listen, you will often repeat the same mistake. It is your choice; purely your choice. We do not try to manipulate or control the outcome. We sit back diligently surveying the situation with your best interest at heart and make the determination for the right action.

If, however, we feel that the lesson to be learned far outweighs our communicating right action, we may withhold the solution. Why? So we can help you in far greater ways than by just giving you the easy way out. Sometimes you need to learn and you need to learn the hard way. Why? Because it is a significantly important and valuable lesson for you and by stopping the lesson, we stop your growth and your growth is most key to all humanity progressing.

We want you to grow and excel and experience life to the fullest. We want you to be happy and healthy, have love and honor and hope. We want you to be in your highest and best place at all times, but sometimes the situation dictates otherwise. Or, to put it another way, the highest and best place happens to be learning the lesson. Why? Because it appears that lesson is significant to your growth and development in the spiritual realm. The spiritual realm being most significant here.

You acquire pain in your life often because you do not listen and you do not learn. Learning lessons can sometimes be difficult, but you should approach the lesson with the idea that if you learn it quickly, you can stop the pain quicker and the solution will be there waiting for you as soon as you are ready to adhere to it.

You need not struggle any longer than necessary. If you approached each and every dilemma with the idea that there is a lesson to be learned and asked yourself *What is it?*, you may move through problems more quickly than at any previous time. You have only to look within to determine the cause and the cause will reveal itself. You need only to look to yourself for the solution and it will be there.

We (I, Michael the Archangel, and all God's angels) are here to assist you in your lessons as well. We don't like to see you suffer and are here to support you in your time of need. Ask and we are there to assist. Listen and we are there with solutions. But look within and determine what is causing you to attract a particular problem and you will do more for your advancement than any of us can. When you can determine why you are attracting a particular type of problem, you can do more for your growth and the growth of mankind than our assistance can. Sometimes our assistance is a permanent fix, at other times it is only a bandage. If you look within yourself and determine why or how you may have created a situation to learn the lesson attached to it, you will have a better chance to not repeat or attract the same scenario or experience in the future. Learn to recognize and let go of situations quickly and you will speed up the process of overcoming problems in your life.

Problems will become easier and easier to solve once you take this approach. You will stop needing to be so attached to being a victim and will look at the opportunity for growth. The quicker you find that solution—the cause—the level of difficulty and the number of problems you have to deal with will lessen.

CHAPTER TWELVE

Do You Want Peace?

We have come a long way here in conversation and now let us get down to some nitty gritty. *How do I change my life in these changing times?* That is the question that comes up in the minds of countless individuals. You ask this day in and day out not satisfied with the lives you are currently living. Sad but true. There are a handful of you, it seems, that are really satisfied. Why? As I said earlier, expectations are a big cause of the problem. The other, the most important and significant, is your relationship to God, your Creator, and the Source of all your supply.

This individual, if you can call Him that, is behind it all. He has it all and He knows it all. You all are a demonstration of a vision He had a long, long time ago. You have manifested in many forms, but over time have come to be who you are today. And, who are you? You are the children of God. You are the individuals that were created by God. You are here to do God's work in one way or another. You cannot escape this fact. This is where you came from and this is what you are here to do.

The problem so many of you have is that you cannot accept this fact. You have been fighting it for eons of time. You think you can actually change this reality. You cannot. It is what it is. You cannot change it. What you can do, however, is accept it. Choose to accept it. I can't begin to tell you how much easier your lives will become if you just accept that fact. It is what it is. Believe it or not, you all were and have been created by God. He exists and is as real as you are today. No matter what you do, you can't change that fact.

But why don't many of you accept or believe it? Because of control. You feel you lose control when you feel someone else has more power over you than you have over yourself. That lack of control scares you so much you don't even begin to realize its power over you. You are all victims of fear, no matter how much money or power you think you have. We know, because we see and hear your inner thoughts and those fears that abound and permeate the actions that you take.

But why run from them? Why not embrace and accept them? Why must you operate from a fear of God and a lack of control? Because you do not realize how much control you really do have. You have the power to control circumstances by just being and accepting. When you choose to be who you are and accept what God has given, you will have so much more than you could possibly imagine by your inability to control the circumstances around you. If you let go of control, you would have so much more than you could ever imagine. You would have it right here and right now. But your fear stands in the way of this acceptance. You cannot be who you are because you do not feel it is enough. You do not have enough because you do not feel it is possible, so you try to control the little you have. You hold so tight that nothing has the power to come or go in your life so you stop all possible flow from expressing itself in your life and, therefore, you stop the ability to receive what is good and right and perfect for you, which, by the way, is abundant in the eyes of the Lord.

God has big plans for you. You have little ones. Some of you with egos the size of some buildings, are probably some of the smallest thinkers around. You may think you are big thinkers with the ability to manipulate and control thousands of people and millions of dollars, but in the scheme of the world at large you are like little ants running this way and that, trying to control the little you can get a hold of to feel better about yourselves in some small way. Do you think we do not notice why you do what you do or how you accomplish it? Do you think God doesn't notice your motives? Who do you think you are kidding? You only delude yourself.

You have come a long way as a society and are moving at light speed in many realms. But there are too many of you still struggling.

Those of you with money are struggling with self-worth in one form or another—family issues, for example. Those of you with good family structures are struggling with money as another example.

All of you struggle in one form or another. Would you like to stop the struggle in your life? Would you like peace in your life? Peace in the world? *Really?* I'm asking you to stop and really think about it. Do you want peace in your life and in the world? If you are continuing to read this next sentence without stopping for five minutes to really digest what I am asking, you do not have a clue. The reason I say that so profoundly is that when you can't even take the time to digest a question of that magnitude, you are demonstrating a life without peace and are clueless as to how to effectually change the outcome.

Do you want peace? I ask you again. How would your life be different if you had peace permeate all areas of your life? What would it look like? Who would you get to be? What would you be able to do? How would you be able to live? How would your life be different? What would the world look and feel like if there were peace in the world? What would be different?

Do you want peace? Think about it. Really think about it. Would it be worth attaining? Would it be worth it to you to do something about it? Really do something about it? You can have peace. You have so much power; you could bring peace into your own lives and in the world. *Do you want peace for you, your family, your loved ones and the world? Do you want peace?*

CHAPTER THIRTEEN

Many Questions

What is to become of me? Will I die? Is there a heaven? Is there life after death? You ask countless questions. Do you know the answers to all of these questions and more lies within you to be answered at any given time? The universe does not withhold truth from you; you do not listen for the answers. The answers lie within you to all the questions you could possibly ask. We are there to answer. God is there to answer. The answers lie within you already, however, for there is no difference in space and time. You most likely lived before. There has never been a time in history before now that so much is culminating in a particular time and space for certain dynamics to occur. These dynamics are occurring at predestined times throughout history in accordance with a higher plan than you can even imagine. You prescribe to the Bible, for example, from which you garner your truths, but the truths in the Bible are not as thorough and complete as they might appear. There is more than meets the eye to recorded history.

Recorded history is one dimension only. There are many dimensions. You operate in one. We operate in another. Others operate in yet another. There are countless. The world is not so simple as it appears. It is quite complex, I might add. But there is much simplicity nonetheless. The simplicity is in the universal laws that many of you now prescribe to but fall short in practicing. Universal law abounds. It cannot be avoided, fooled, overcome, or tricked. Universal law is universal law. I am not here to prescribe or dictate universal law to you. As I see your struggles,

I am here to give my perspective as how I see it and relate to the world at large. I hear your countless prayers. Many prayers go unanswered because you don't listen for the answer or don't recognize the answer when given. You seem to think the answers to your prayers should be a certain way. Well, often they aren't even close to what you are expecting but the ultimate goal may be achieved nonetheless.

When you pray for something and expect a solution in a certain manner, you often miss the gift or answer to your prayer because it doesn't come the way you expect. You would like a perfect box gift-wrapped and left at your door, but it does not come that way. It often comes in a phone call inviting you to attend an affair, a lunch, a gathering of sorts. When you arrive there, you will notice something or hear something or convey your need or wish to someone and they will open the door to what you need to do in order to bring what you desire into manifestation.

You think money should come out of heaven and miraculously appear in your lap or bank account. It often comes through a job offer, an unexpected contest, and an opportunity to go somewhere, which opens the door to something else. It is all a process and you are waiting for one specific event to occur and that is it. Well, it rarely happens that way if at all. What occurs is that the universe and all its inhabitants hear your prayers and they are aligned in discussion over your request. When they determine the best outcome, they will decide on the best tactic to help you attain the answer to the request you set forth. You would be surprised at how simple or convoluted the solution can be depending on the situation and also depending on your willingness to let go and cooperate.

Your lack of cooperation with our efforts is probably our biggest obstacle in helping you. You are in your own way, *and ours,* so often it's comical. Get out of the way and let us help you! You are frustrated, *and so are we at times,* because we want to help and you do not always make it easy on us. You want, you want, you want. But when it comes to receiving, you block us continuously. You are so clever in blocking us that you don't even realize you are doing it. You have such hidden agendas it's amazing we get through at all.

You all have such trouble manifesting what you desire because you block all the help we are trying to give and give and give. Then, you pray again and then we start the process all over again. Fortunately, for us, it is not a big part of our day because we don't relate to time and space as you do. But you are all funny to watch at times and we sometimes do get tired of trying to overcome the same obstacles with you over and over.

You are funny when you say you want x, y, or z. Then you specify what, why, and how, and then bargain with us and make it oh so complicated at times. Please just ask and then accept that if it's honest and legal, it will be given to you. Unfortunately, for you, however, it may not be given to you in *your* timeframe. It will be given to you when it's the *right* time and not before. We have your highest and best interests in mind and if you receive what you want prior to your being truly ready for it, you will either block it or sabotage it if you get it.

When you don't express gratitude, we question giving you something for which you aren't grateful. Many of you complain and whine about this and that, and wonder why you don't have what you want. The negativity is blocking you achieving your goals. It's your choice to whine and complain, or change the situation. Changing things isn't always easy for you because you carry eons of thoughts and memories that sabotage your highest and best thoughts and actions. Getting rid of those past memories and thoughts will greatly help your ability to draw forth that which you truly desire. Wallowing in the past, which most of you do to one degree or another, only delays receiving what you desire. You must forget about the past in order to progress.

You have the ability to eliminate the past, which is weighing you down and keeping you from manifesting that which you truly desire. But underneath those desires often lie the thoughts of neediness, lack, limitation, low self-esteem, unworthiness, etc. What comes to mind is a sand pile. You want to build a castle in the sand. You don't have a solid foundation to build upon because the thoughts that are backing up the building process are weak. You move forward and build some, and then your weakness of character comes forth and the castle collapses before it's even built. You struggle and struggle and start again, using the same materials as before and yet you get the same results and wonder why. Or, the other alternative is you stop building and quit. And then what happens? You quit and say it can't be done, you don't have what it takes, it's not possible, it will never happen, it's not meant to be, so on and so forth. You are then reinforcing the negative beliefs you initially attempted to build upon.

Have you ever considered starting a project based on a foundation of clear thinking? Why not determine all the negative thoughts you have before going in and attempting to build your castle? Why not spend some time with yourself determining what could go wrong and how you would feel and what you would do about it, etc? Why not determine what you feel and think about a situation, working through those negative beliefs before embarking on a project? Work out the kinks in your head so you won't have to work out the kinks in the building phase.

You have only to look within to determine how a project will go. Your thoughts will determine the outcome. No thought, unless a good thought, will determine a positive outcome. Unless you have a positive expectation and determination to build the castle you wish, you will be building one on sand at the mercy of the environment and you are the environment.

How you think is the environment upon which your castle and anything else in your life will be built. The results that occur are a direct reflection as to the thoughts that went into creating the castle you build. Clear out the negative thoughts going into the project and you will create a better outcome—no matter what you are trying to create. If you are trying to create anything based and built on false ideas and negative thinking and memories, you will have built something subject to collapse. If you have five pillars and one pillar is rocky because of an unresolved issue, that pillar could be your downfall.

What are the negative thoughts you have about the castle you wish to build? What is stopping you? What do you believe could happen? Where could you go wrong? How do you expect people to feel and react to the castle you are building? Do you expect support? Do you think they will have doubts? If you don't clear out those doubts going in, you will be building your foundation on doubts. Other people's doubts about your ability *will* have an impact on your results. Make sure only those who are supportive and can help you, know what you want to accomplish, create, or attract. Anyone else and you are setting yourself up to be sabotaged. The best-intentioned friends and relatives are your worst enemies at times of creation, most of the time. They have so much misunderstanding and jealousy and doubts and fears that their thoughts alone can sabotage the results you seek. Keep your desires to yourself unless you are guided to share something with someone specifically.

When you tune into yourself, and follow the guidance you seek, you will be led to the people, places, and circumstances aligned to support you in achieving that which you endeavor. You have only to look at yourself to know what to do when and to follow what you receive to get the best outcome possible.

Think about something too long and someone else in the universe will pick up on the idea and run with it. Be proactive and take the idea and run with it at your first possible chance, as the ideas in the universe are abundant and not always yours. You are often divinely guided by thoughts and ideas that could create the answers to your prayers, and yet you miss them because you feel inadequate in some manner in your ability to carry forth on the idea. If an idea is given to you, you will also be given the resources to manifest the idea.

If you have an idea, you may have a whole team of experts in heaven ready, willing, and able to assist you every step of the way. Just because angels and other beings of light around you cannot be seen by most individuals, does not mean that they aren't there capable of assisting you. The heavenly experts may not be able to do certain physical things for you, but they can lead and inspire you to right action and put the appropriate people and other resources in your path. But, *you* must seize the opportunities and follow through on them. We cannot do that part for you. That would stump your growth. There is a reason you specifically have been given certain ideas. It is up to you to execute them, but you wouldn't be given the idea without the resources ultimately to make it happen for you. You have only to trust in this fact and move forward on the next "good" idea that comes your way. You have only to listen and to act. Acting is key. You can have all the good ideas in the world but if you don't take proper action on them, you will not have achieved anything. You will remain stuck continuing to pray for a solution, too stubborn to recognize that the solution has been given unto you already.

Countless ideas have come to pass that could have made you wealthy, but instead make someone else so. Other ideas are still available to you because the universe is abundant, but you may have missed your chance to seize a certain opportunity by your lack of action. So, the next time you receive guidance, an idea or an inspiration, seize it without judging how, when, and where.

CHAPTER FOURTEEN

The Solution Lies Within You

Over and over again, people struggle and blame themselves, God, and others for circumstances they feel are beyond their control. At this time, like no other time in history, it is easier to take responsibility and clear the cause of those problems. It doesn't really matter what the cause of the problem is as long as you let it go. I know it sounds easy but is more difficult in practice.

We are here to help. Rather than play a victim of circumstance, become aware of the fact that the solution lies within you and that we are here to help you if you ask us. We have to be asked. We don't intervene without your asking us. We are readily available at any time to offer our assistance if you only ask.

What we need you to do is be willing to look within and acknowledge that the cause of your dilemma lies within and accept 100% responsibility for it, without self-blame or admonishment. Just accept that the cause lies within, accept 100% responsibility for it, and ask that we assist you in releasing it.

We may have to work with you in a procedural manner to get to the cause and at times we can remove it, if you are close enough to the cause and its accessibility. What we often must do, however, is show you the path to understanding the cause. Frequently, there is a lesson attached to it that first must be learned. If you do not learn the lesson, you have lost the value the dilemma has to teach you.

In other cases, you may not benefit from the lesson because you already possess the knowledge but are bearing the burden of your forebears who did not learn the lesson and passed it on to you. Frequently, you suffer because of circumstances outside of you, but the cause still lies within for you to release. If there is no lesson attached for you to learn, it is much easier for you to release the cause from within and allow yourself to move on to experience what is right and perfect for you and yours. However, if you are stubborn and need to learn a lesson for which you have not been willing to take responsibility, you may have to learn the lesson again via personal experience. If at that time, you have a greater willingness to take responsibility and look to yourself as the cause, we may be able to assist you in rectifying the situation so that it will never occur for you again.

Once you have learned a lesson, you will not have to repeat a situation. Whatever negative experience you have can be released permanently from your makeup if you clear it 100% from within yourself. Those of you who continue to experience the same situation repeatedly are victims of your own ignorance, as you have been unwilling to see your part in the play in this instance.

Your life is very much like a play. There is predestination involved as well as free will. You are given a framework from which to operate and grow, and experience the life you were meant to have and yet you can sabotage it, deny your good, and create something other than the original plan. Nothing is written in stone. However, there is a framework from which to operate. You were meant to live a certain life, learning specific lessons for this particular period of time. Those lessons can be hard learned or easily learned, depending on your willingness to pay attention and accept responsibility. You chose the lessons you wished to learn during this lifetime very much the way you choose a specific college curriculum. You can't avoid the curriculum, but you can make it a lot easier on yourself and those around you by a willingness to learn the lessons set before you as quickly and as painlessly as possible.

If you are repeating a negative experience, then you have been held back, much like in school, in order for you to learn the lesson before moving on to the next grade. If you want to move on, you choose to work harder at your lesson and make sure you get everything out of the lesson, as thoroughly as possible, in order to pass the test and move on to the next class. You have a reprieve—time off and then the opportunity to take another class. That is why life is up and down, up and down. You may have chosen more than one lesson during a lifetime or you may have chosen to become a teacher. If you have chosen to become a teacher, you may or may not have lessons to learn, or as many lessons, but you have chosen to come to be of service. You are a student, a teacher, or both; it's your choice. But the choice was made before you came to this planet. You chose to be here at this time doing what you are doing.

Your path may deviate somewhat, but the ultimate purpose and curriculum remains the same throughout. You cannot deviate from that initial role you chose because your life was orchestrated to support that role. Embrace the role you chose; you chose it for a reason. When you chose it, you had the best intentions and the overall picture of the impact it would have on your growth overall. It is what *you wanted* for yourself. No one else made the choices for you; however, you had input from others who wished to support you in making the right choices. It did not happen by accident. You actually had a team of experts, such as guidance counselors, who assisted you in making the choices for your role in this lifetime. You chose willingly and with ample assistance. Embrace this idea and your life will become much easier because you will no longer resist what persists. You will recognize that the opportunity of learning a new lesson is upon you and you will eagerly seek to find its core and benefit, thereby alleviating much of the stress of the lesson.

Your lessons will be much less challenging and much more rewarding when you approach them in this light. Look for the opportunity for growth, knowing that you chose this path with your best interests at heart. Know that it is for your own good and then look for the good in every situation. Look at all situations as an opportunity, or you will miss the gift in each and every opportunity put in your path. Embrace your path—because *you* chose it. Release the anxiety, knowing that it is happening in order to advance your higher good and the good of others. You must seek the lesson, learn from it, release it, and then move on to a more fulfilling and rewarding life for you and for all others.

Every lesson you learn impacts another. You cannot avoid it. If you learn the lesson, others will suffer less as well because as *you* learn more of the lesson, so do others. You are all connected and cannot do anything in isolation. All are impacted by your willingness to learn and look within. Whenever you take responsibility and take the lesson to heart, there will be fewer and fewer who have to endure the same lesson. What a gift you can give to humanity by being diligent in your schoolwork. Learn, and you shall impact the world. Avoid and deny, and you will cause yourself to be held back and will hold back all humanity in the process.

You see, you do make a difference—a much bigger difference that you could ever imagine. You can change the world, one lesson at a time; one good choice at a time. Be effective and conscious in the world in which you live, knowing clearly that you impact all around you and those you don't even see. You are not alone in this endeavor. You are all in this together.

You, who sit in judgment of the mistakes of others, may or may not have already experienced that lesson. But it is not for you to judge. If you can help another individual realize their lesson quicker, it will make it easier for all. But don't do this out of righteousness or arrogance, do it out of love for yourself and all humanity. By caring for another during their time of struggle, you can empower them. Do not enable them, but empower them. Do not take the lesson from them, as the lesson is what they need. By providing the solution, you sometimes deny them their growth. By denying their growth, you also deny all of the benefits of the lesson.

You cannot do for another what they must do for themselves, but you can be there to bring light to the situation and give support. If you are divinely guided to assist, then do so lovingly because that may be where the lesson lies for you. Being of service to another may be the lesson you need to embrace for yourself. You do not know. When you listen to the voice within, you will know when it is appropriate to help and when it is not. For instance, you may be guided to give to the beggar on the street or you may not. Do not judge another for their generosity or lack thereof. Therein lies the lesson: each individual's path is different. Should you choose to impose your will and judgment on another, you will only cause yourself more harm and more negativity. Each negative impact you incur has a negative impact on the world.

Each judgment you make creates harm in the world, and often most pronouncedly for yourself. Your judgments are a mere reflection of yourself because the flaw will most assuredly lie within. However, if you judge a situation objectively in order to ascertain your role and how you can contribute to the cause at large, you will then be discerning and choose right action based on the right direction inspired from within.

When you sit in judgment, assuming that another is wrong and you are right, you are usually a victim of ignorance of your own flaws. In that case, you will be given the lesson to recognize those flaws within yourself. At no time will you avoid being judged if you sit in judgment of others. If you stop judging others, you will not be judged yourself. Judgment is a cruel game we play on ourselves because we are always made to pay for the judgments we make.

CHAPTER FIFTEEN

Fighting Life's Battles

There is continuous fighting going on in the world as people blame each other for this and that. Do you know how ancient some of these battles are that are being fought today? You have no idea what is really the cause in these situations. But instead of stopping to look at and address the cause, you send out your men, your sons, your daughters, your husbands and wives, mothers and fathers to do battle. Who do they battle. Yourselves. You have no idea that you are externally fighting yourselves as you make your way through the world to resolve issues that lie within.

The issues you fight about are no more mysterious than your own thoughts. If you decide to clean up your own thoughts, you would clean up the world. If you want to stop fighting, stop the turmoil within. That is where it starts. You are the cause of war. No one else. If you think the cause of war lies outside of you or on the other side of the world, you are sadly mistaken. You are all at cause; each and every one of you.

You think, not I. It's not my battle. But it is. It is. It is within your own heart and mind. No one is separated from another. If it lies in one, it lies in another; it lies in all. You cannot escape this dynamic no matter how righteous you are. If you think you can avoid this truth, you only perpetuate the battles that exist throughout the world throughout time. There is no time like the present to start to take responsibility for them. Could you imagine if you really wanted peace and took responsibility for the state of affairs that exist today, what power you would have to create peace on earth?

But most of you are too busy to care, wrapped up in your own drama, running this way and that not taking the time to look at yourself and take responsibility for the world at large. It is your fault; you are to blame. Why? Because the cause lies within and the opportunity exists for you to clear it, but you choose to ignore it as well as not take responsibility, the problems persist and the battles continue.

Would you rather stop and think about what is going on in the world and acknowledge the cause that lies within and change it by taking responsibility and letting it go? Or would you rather sacrifice human life, live in fear, and continue as you have? You know it's your choice. It is up to you. What do you choose? Peace on earth or this madness that continues year after year, century after century, lifetime after lifetime?

How do you change it?, you ask. By accepting responsibility, asking forgiveness, and letting it go. Each and every one of you needs to take responsibility for the state of affairs on your planet. No one else is responsible but you. Why blame others? Why not take the opportunity to fix it and set it right? It is within you to change the world. Do not wait for someone else to do it. They may never get around to it. If they are stuck in old patterns that perpetuate a thought and a reaction, would you prefer leaving it up to them to determine the outcome of the world within which you live, or take responsibility for your part in it and release the cause into God's hands, who has the power of all behind Him.

He can make a difference, as can you. You wait for Him to do the job. But it is up to you to clean up the planet and the state of affairs on it. Not Him. He did not create the havoc that exists; you did. You did—this lifetime; every lifetime. Not God, not I. We will help you and support you in this endeavor to clean up the mess you have created, but you have to do your part and take responsibility for it. As long as you blame another, you perpetuate the battle. The battle lies within; not without. You are at cause. Not your neighbor. Not this religious sector or another. No one is right or off the hook on this one.

You are *all* responsible, each and every one of you. Would you prefer to blame the neighbor, the guy across the street, or across the world?

What does it matter? You have only to mind your own business. But it is your business if you want peace on the planet. If you don't want peace on the planet, then ignore your responsibility in the matter and allow your family, friends and coworkers to perish, become maimed and suffer unnecessary harm because you prefer to keep your head in the sand. Denial does wonders for the world at large. It keeps everything status quo, offering you the opportunity to return lifetime after lifetime until you wake up and take responsibility for the state of affairs that exist today.

Once you get this, the whole world will be different. The Shangri-La that you dreamt about long ago would become a reality rather than impossibility. You have only to change yourself in order to change the world. Which is easier? Looking at yourself or sending your children off into battle? So far, you have found it easier to allow yourself and your loved ones to go off into battle than to look within.

Why? Because no one wants to know the crud, the mess that lies within. No one wants to recognize and accept the past as it is; a troubled soul that has floundered and fought and created and mis-created all that exists. You have only to look at yourself and all the ugliness that lies within to clean up all the ugliness that lies without. All the negative experiences expressed in the world, start from the negative experiences that lie within. The thoughts and memories you carry within are what determines the world without. You have only to change the thoughts within to change the world.

Thinking that fighting the battles on the outside are easier requires the fight to continue until the responsibility for it is acknowledged, accepted, and forgiven from within. Until you forgive yourself and resolve the battles within, the battles throughout the world will continue. Wouldn't it make sense to stop for a moment and look within and let go of all the battles within, rather than continue the battle and the demonstration of it throughout the world?

CHAPTER SIXTEEN

Search For God Within

Many struggle in the world trying to find your right place. Many of you feel a higher calling or a desire for something more. What you seek is your connection to your Source. Once you have that, you will be guided to your right place. Before that, you flounder going from this to that searching for something more. You look in the outer realm for everything thinking this or that may give you the fulfillment you search for and what you search for is your connection to God.

God is found within you, not in things. You search in things, in activities, in jobs, in people for that which is inside of you and has been all along. If I can get you to go inside once and for all, you will experience a marked difference in your life on the outside. The outside reflects what is going on inside. If you address the inside, you fix the outside automatically.

Unfortunately, for many of you it's not as easy as it sounds. So many of you face unresolved issues and those issues keep you stymied and hold you back. Addressing those issues once and for all will help you move forward in leaps and bounds rather than big steps forward and many backward as you so often do. Those steps forward give you hope and those thoughts within that have constantly held you back revert to bringing you back time and time again because they were never resolved. Brushing things (feelings in particular) under the carpet does not work. It only perpetuates bringing you further pain again and again.

If you learn to address situations as they arise the first time, you will go a long way to eliminating their recurrence in the future. What you commonly do, however, is ignore them hoping they will go away, only to find that the circumstances and feelings surrounding them will reoccur. No longer will you have to experience things that you are done with. If you complete your past, you will no longer need to bring it forward to heal it completely. Complete your experiences and learn from them immediately, and you will not be forced to revisit them.

You repeat your negative experiences over and over again due to your lack of willingness to address them adequately the first time they surface. I trust you'd prefer to not relive negative experiences. Well, if you would really like to avoid them, analyze each scenario as it occurs the first time and determine how to better handle the situation the next time from all sides of the story. Don't just look at yourself as a victim, as you are never a victim. You are only attracting a situation because you have some part in its creation. If you had no reason to attract it, it would not occur for you. What I see happen over and over again is that people have experiences that they do not like but rather than look at themselves and their part in attracting those particular circumstances, they look at the world as *doing it to them*. Therefore, they have not taken responsibility for the situation and will again attract that situation to them until they do. Most often, you just accept blame as if you are unworthy of good, or blame circumstances or others for your problems. Neither is true. We, each and every one of us, are responsible for our circumstances. Nothing has to do with unworthiness or blame of another.

What you need to do in these circumstances is to stop and accept that the cause of the situation lies within, and that each and everyone of you have the power to make a difference in the future outcome by doing so. Should you desire to not repeat the current circumstances you face, take full responsibility for them. If you do not, it will stay alive only to repeat itself again until you get the message.

Circumstances do not change until you do. You can change yourself easier than circumstances. Change your beliefs first and foremost about the circumstances; look at yourself first and foremost as the key to the enfoldment of all circumstances in your life and your power to change the circumstances you face grows dramatically. You can change your outer world by changing your inner world. Look at yourself before you look at changing your outer world. You will be amazed at how quickly you can change your outer experiences by changing your beliefs, taking responsibility for your outcomes and moving forward in a responsible manner. No one can change your circumstances quicker than you can. No one.

Take the opportunity to recognize how powerful you really are in your own life. You are not a victim any more than I am. I may have a light body within which to move about easier than you do, but you are just as powerful if you would understand the power within you and how to access it. Recognizing that power first and foremost will put you light years ahead of others who do not recognize and accept it. You have only to look within to access all the power in the universe. You have the power to change that universe by your willingness to change yourself. You can change anything you desire if you apply yourself long enough by going within and taking responsibility.

Can you take responsibility? Are you willing to take responsibility for your own problems as well as those that occur in the world? I think not. Most of you will not. You much prefer sitting in judgment of others, putting your head in the sand, blaming others, all acts of cowardice and ineffectiveness. How easy is it is to sit back and play victim, blame others and sit in judgment, and whine about life as a whole. How much easier is it for you all to blame God, others, and anyone or anything else rather than to look at yourself?

The only problem with that is it only perpetuates the problem. If you *really* want to get over your problems, take responsibility for them.

CHAPTER SEVENTEEN

Change Yourself: Change The World

The struggles of the world lie dormant within each individual, waiting for someone to address them; anyone. It could be you. You could be the one who could make the difference in the world. *You*! You have the power to make a significant difference by being who you are and doing what is divinely right and guided for you. If you each did what you were meant to do, you could change the world significantly. You need not wait for someone else to do it for you or for the world. You have the power to significantly change and enhance the world by identifying all that lies within you that doesn't empower you or the world. By being all you were meant to be and taking 100% responsibility for yourself and for your circumstances, you have the power to make significant change. As mentioned before, you can change the world by changing yourself and the limiting beliefs and sabotaging thoughts that lie within (sometimes for centuries). You old souls are the guiltiest and have the hardest time because your baggage is endless at times. You drag with you countless lifetimes of beliefs and habits that riddle your lives today.

Thoughts that have impacted your life for eons continue to impact you and the world now. You need not carry these burdens with you any longer. They no longer serve you or empower the world at large. The world at large needs you to take responsibility for yourself, your actions, your beliefs, the thoughts you carry and have carried for eons of time.

Those thoughts often hold you down and keep the progress of the world from occurring.

Can you let go of those limiting beliefs so the world can evolve? All mankind is waiting for one, for anyone of you to evolve by letting go of the past and those limiting beliefs you carry and hold so dear. You operate your whole world out of those beliefs, and compounded with the limiting beliefs of others, you sabotage yourself, each other and the world at large. Can you change yourself to change the world? You bet you can. Is it easy? For some, sometimes; sometimes, not at all.

It can be difficult at times to look within and identify the thoughts that hold you back and limit you. Sometimes only others can bring them to your attention. Watch what goes on around you. That is your evidence of what you believe. The life you live is the one you envision out of your beliefs, limiting or not. What you experience is what you believe to be true. If you do not experience a life that you truly desire, then you are demonstrating limiting beliefs. By identifying and changing those limiting beliefs, you can change your life and the world at large. As you change, so does the world.

Do not wait for the world to change. It will not until you do. If you want the world to change, then you must change. Start with you. If you are not happy with what you see demonstrated in the world around you, then start looking at yourself first and foremost. Start with what you can change. Yourself. You can change you. No one else can change you. Until you change yourself, your world will not change.

Do not wait for someone else to change or the world to change. Change yourself and your world will change before your eyes. You will see profound change in the world, when you change profoundly. You will see little change in the world, if you change a little. Which would you prefer? Life as you have seen and experienced it thus far or a life full of wonder and joy?

It is time for you to identify the world as you would prefer it as well as the key thoughts creating the life as you are experiencing it. Once you have identified both aspects, you can begin to move forward to generate your life as you would prefer it and watch the world change before your very eyes. Do not wait for the world to change. Change the world.

CHAPTER EIGHTEEN

Take Right Action

The longer you wait to make the right choices, the more difficult your life will become. Each time you choose the path of least resistance, your life unfolds in a new and different way. Each time you choose a path divinely chosen for you, your life unfolds in a new and different way. What you need to adhere to if you wish your life to unfold as it should to meet your highest goals and desires, is to ask your divine self what is right and perfect for you.

Each and every day, each and every decision can be made from asking yourself for the perfect and right solution, choice or direction. No one has to guess, second guess, wonder, live in indecision, doubt, etc, when asking your higher self for the right and perfect answer. All this lies within. You think that you have to figure things out. You don't. You only have to ask. You have to ask yourself and the higher power within for the answer and you will always get the right answer for where you are at that particular time. The answer may change as you do, but for the interim, the answer will be right and perfect for that moment.

Each and every moment countless activities, thoughts, and beliefs change the universe at large. Each and every one of you impacts the universe as a whole. Each time you flounder, the universe flounders. Each time you make the right and perfect decision, the universe strengthens as a whole. If you want to impact the world, make right and perfect decisions for who you are in each and every instance. Stop running around looking here and there for the answers, go within, make right choices and all will be well all of the time.

You think you do not matter. You think your actions do not make a difference. Your actions make a difference in countless ways and in numerous directions. Your actions, your inactions, your decisions and your indecisions all impact each other and the world at large. Do you want to make a difference in the world? Then start with yourself. Look at yourself and your responsibility in the world and in the scheme of things. All have a ripple effect. Nothing escapes this factor. Do you want to make a difference in the world? Then take responsibility for yourself and your contribution to the effect your life has upon the world.

Look at yourself and yourself alone in this. You have the responsibility to take right action and if you do not, you have a responsibility to clean up the mess you created by not adhering to right action. How do you know when it's right action? You ask or move along in a higher state of natural consciousness choosing wisely from the way you feel in a higher state of conscious awareness. Do not succumb to fear and doubt, as they will set you down the wrong path. Choose again if you choose unwisely. Correct and set aright all wrong action as quickly as possible and you will see the difference in your life as well as in the lives of others.

There are no accidents that you are with those whom you are with. You have impacted each other's lives before and will continue to do so as long as you act consciously or unconsciously in each and every moment. It's your choice, however, if you act consciously or unconsciously.

Act out of integrity and the experience will be an integrious one. Act out of fear and it will be a fear-based decision and result. Act out of faith and doors will open for you and all concerned. If you limit yourself, you limit others. If you have faith, others will have faith. If you get right results, others will get right results.

When you think of yourself and yourself alone acting out of right and perfect decisions, all those around you will benefit. It may not always be seemingly at first, but it will be right and perfect for all concerned. As you come in to your right place, others are allowed and encouraged to fall into theirs. Once all are in their right place, the world will be in balance and harmony. Once the world is in balance and harmony, the door opens for others to be in their right place. As each planet gets into their right place in the universe, the universe becomes in balance. Once the universe becomes in balance, the next universe will become in balance so on and so far. The results are endless but they start with you.

You have the power to change your world, the world at large, and the universe as a whole as you become increasingly dedicated to being in the right place at the right time. Once you take your right place in the world and in the universe, all else has a fighting chance of doing the same. Start with you; start now. There is no time like the present. Seize the moment; seize the opportunity. The world needs you and your dedication to yourself. There is not a moment to be missed. Time is of the essence for each of you to take your rightful place in the universe. The time is now. Please do yourselves a favor by taking your rightful place. Do it now. That is all.

CHAPTER NINETEEN

Self-Limiting Behavior

What is to become of you? That is up to you. You think you have no power. You have greater power than you can ever imagine. Use it to your benefit. That is not to say use your power to win over others and create a win/lose situation. This is nothing of the sort. The power I speak of is the power of the universe; the power of God, the I within. You have great power to accomplish all that you can imagine. You limit your power by the thoughts you think that create the results you experience in your life. Because your thoughts are ones of lack and limitation, your experiences are such.

If you choose again, knowing that the power within can create all reality, you may wish to identify the limiting thoughts you possess that inhibit the results you truly desire. The results you desire are innately accurate and appropriate and possible for you. What you do, however, is sabotage those results and experiences from occurring because you limit the thoughts, which create the outcome you least desire. Or, you move forward toward the idea you desire and sabotage the actual attainment of that which you desire because an old and outmoded thought creeps in and sabotages those desired results. You are all the same. No one escapes this dynamic in any area of life. Some have certain areas handled and accomplished while they lack in others. Those areas in which you are not gaining the results you desire, are the ones you need to identify and address to release the self-sabotaging and limiting results you are achieving.

You have the power to change your results by changing the dynamics of your thought processes, which only you have the capacity to change. We can help you but only you can change them by your willingness to identify them and let them go. It is your choice, always your choice. You live in a world of limitation because of lack somewhere in your consciousness. It's not that you always feel undeserving, but on some level you do because of past experiences and beliefs that you carry.

Should you desire to change the effects of your life, you need to identify where you are limiting yourself. The guilt that you carry can be centuries and lifetimes old and yet it has such a strong hold on you that you perpetuate a negative experience of long ago lifetime after lifetime until the day you choose to let it go. Your past often rules your present and to the degree you do not clearly see it, you allow it to continue to affect your life, or you would make every effort to let it go. You need not be ruled from your past and until now you have often lived your life out of your past.

Your past dictates your future (and your most precious present) by living the results of the past over and over again. If you learn to let go of the past, forgive yourself and others, you can move on to create greater and greater heights, bigger and bigger joys, and more life worth living and loving.

You often suffer not of your own doing but by ignorance of the past and of the reality at hand. You live your life guilty of pasts long done, experiences of your ancestry and people long gone who unfortunately still dictate the results you are experiencing. Let it go. Once and for all, let it go. Live in the now. Live the life you desire. Let go of the past fully and completely so you are not a victim of your own ignorance, deeds long done and gone, and your family's disappointments and experiences. Live for today, so your tomorrow will be full, complete and on purpose.

Let go of the past so your past does not dictate your future. Your life is worth living. Only you can live it to the fullest. No one can live it for you. No one can fix it for you. Only you can do that. You have the power within to do all the necessary work of healing the past and putting it to rest once and for all so you, as well as the rest of your family and the world, can move on.

You hold yourself back and those in your family, as well as the rest of the world by your unwillingness to look at yourself, your limiting thoughts and beliefs, and letting them go. Once you let them go, you can put to rest your past, your family's past and allow the world to be a better place by your lack of resistance to move on from the past. Live for the future by living fully in the present. Live for today fully so your tomorrow is perfect. Your tomorrow is here soon enough. As long as you live in the past, you stay in the past with no room for a brighter future. Move on by letting go. Experience life to the fullest by letting go of a past that's long gone. Living from yesterday is too difficult. Live for today and tomorrow so your life is worth living and you're contributing. No longer live from the past wherein your guilt, your past behaviors, and your experiences are limiting your valuable future.

You cannot fully contribute to the world by living in the past and not fully living in the present. The time has come for all mankind to live in their right place, do their right work, and live the life they were meant to live—not one of dragging the past forward lifetime after lifetime, but one of freedom and joy. Live that life and all will be well, happy and joyful.

Live the life of your past and all you do is carry forth the pain inflicted then into the future and your precious present. Let it all go and live-and-let-live, and all will have a fighting chance of being in their right place for their highest good. No one need carry his or her baggage further into the future than they have already. It serves no purpose. No one suffers more than the one carrying the baggage, but all suffer in one way or another.

You limit the world by limiting yourself. Continue as you have been and life will continue as it has been. Please let it go for yourself, for me, and for all mankind. Change your thoughts, your limitations, and your patterns and all else will change in the process.

CHAPTER TWENTY

Your Rightful Place In The Universe

Although a long time in coming, all are about ready to move into their right places in society and in the world. There is great movement in preparing people to take their rightful place. There is enormous dissatisfaction. People are unsettled and are questioning everything. They are upset because they feel that their lives are not their own. They are running in this direction and that, not sure why but feeling compelled to do so. The mores of society are bogging them down, and they see no way out. Often they cry out to me, to us, wanting a solution, and a better way, but they do not expect an answer so they do not wait for one.

The world is in an upheaval bringing all back into eventual balance. Although it does not appear that way, that is the way it is. The shake up, if you will, is that the world wants to be balanced, as do her inhabitants. All must be in their rightful place if all is to be in balance.

It is no longer appropriate to do whatever you can to make a buck. It is imperative that you do the right thing that you were meant to do this lifetime. All of you who choose money over your right livelihood will suffer even more than before. You are frequently suffering just because you are choosing money over your rightful place. It is time you moved into your rightful place or you will continue to suffer. It is your choice, always your choice. Money is a by-product, however, you make it your most important focus. It should not and should never be your focus. Your focus should always be, no matter what, what is the right thing you are supposed to do? What did you choose for yourself before coming into this world? That is what you need to be asking yourself.

You need to be clear and know what it is you were supposed to do during this lifetime. *Ask yourself what you desired as a child as well as what you are drawn to now?* You have been sidetracked long enough. The longer you choose to remain off your path, the harder it will become for you in the long term. The quicker you can rebalance your life by choosing what it is you were meant to do, the easier your life will become long term. I realize that in any time of transition, there is adjustment, but, I think as a whole, you will be pleasantly surprised that it will go much smoother than you anticipate. You will be frightened thinking you will have to give up certain things, as they do not fit within this next context somehow, but believe me they are not worth giving up your path for completely. The closer to your target you become, the happier you will be. Money will follow those who choose to be on the right path. However, it may not be the same amount of money nor will it come in the same way as you anticipate.

You need to let go of your ideas about money and where it comes from. You look at it and serve it as master. It is master over most of your lives. If you learn to let it go, it will be much easier to receive. You will see. The more you remember God is the source of our supply, the easier it will be to let go of what you believe to be the current source of your supply—your current employer, etc. This avenue of supply may be of use and may have served its purpose but it's imperative now for you to take your rightful place in the world and do the job you were meant to do. If you are unhappy in your current employment, there is a good chance it is not meant for you. You need to be in your right place, doing the work you were meant to do as soon as possible.

If you need additional training, research, or planning, that is fine. The sooner you begin, the happier you will be. Just getting on your right path will open doors for you. The universe as a whole will help support you as you move into your right place. Once you have decided to move into your rightful job, the universe will open the right doors and bring you whatever resources necessary to bring you fulfillment. This is not a matter to be taken lightly. It is imperative for you to take your rightful place in the world. Time is of the essence and the longer you procrastinate, the harder it will be for all involved.

By taking up the job of another, you prohibit them from being in their place. Let go of your fear and you will begin to have the right doors open before you. Continue to stay in a place that is wrong for you and you will continue to experience more unpleasantness in one form or another.

The time has come for you to take a stand in who you are and what you were meant to do. There is no time like the present to begin this process of identifying what you feel talented in and naturally drawn to do. Let go of all your limiting beliefs about going for that completely and quickly, and begin to take the steps necessary toward the achievement of that goal. You will find that it is much easier than you imagined. It always is. People are often surprised by how easy it is to do their right job. It is so easy to them, because they are using the talents innate to them; they often feel unworthy of pay.

If it is easy, it is still worth being paid well for it. You need not struggle to be paid well. You can do well and have it easy at the same time. Those of you who choose to struggle in order to feel your worth are deluding yourselves and making a grave mistake. Work does not need to be hard or a struggle and you can be paid very well for work that is easy and fun. It is preconceived notions like this that keep people stuck in the wrong jobs and throwing the planet out of balance because of it. It is time to take that stand, do what is rightfully yours to do, and be at peace because you made the right choice.

CHAPTER TWENTY-ONE

What You Think Is What You Get

You have come to a place in time where time is of the essence. Every move you make and every thought you think has immediate impact. There is no longer a lag time between what you think and your result. You are demonstrating daily what you believe. It is evident in all that surrounds you. What you tend to not realize is that you are creating the results in your life.

The problem lies in you not realizing that and instead complaining about what is not working instead. The world has changed such that time has been shortened or expedited. You no longer can be willy nilly about your thoughts. They are imperative to your outcome. What you think is what you get. If you are not getting the results you seek, you are thinking the wrong thoughts. You, however, may not be fully aware of those thoughts. Some are deeply imbedded and need assistance to ascertain. Nonetheless, those thoughts are dictating your present and future. If you would like change in your present and future, you need to change the thoughts you are thinking.

If you don't know what they are, write about a subject. Just take a paper and write down all the thoughts that come and are related to that subject. For example, "I'm not getting….". Write down all your beliefs about that subject and why you believe you aren't or can't get what you want. You might discover some hidden thoughts sabotaging those results you seek.

Once you have figured out what thoughts may be inhibiting your results, change the thoughts. Pick a new phrase or belief system and practice repeating that until you own the statement or belief. Keep doing that with all thoughts that conflict with the goals at hand. Once you have eliminated the thoughts that sabotage your results, your outer experience will reflect your new ideas.

Reprogramming yourself is crucial, although not as easy as we would like, as some thoughts are deeply imbedded from lifetimes of reaffirmation of those beliefs and experiences. Keep at it, however, as there is no other way to change your outer experience than by changing your inner expression of them.

Once you begin to see the power of your thoughts and the words you speak, you can begin to be more conscious in your choices. You will begin to experience how powerful they truly are and begin to use them to your advantage, creating the ideal life that you desire as opposed to one that comes from a default from lifetimes of experiences and listening to others and their beliefs assuming they are right. If the results they speak about are not what you seek for yourself, do not listen to them and begin creating your own experience by choosing the thoughts that support that which you desire.

The more you do this, the more you will begin to experience the results you desire more consistently. The more consistently you achieve the results you desire, the more powerful you will become. The more powerful you become, the more you will experience exactly what you desire.

CHAPTER TWENTY-TWO

The Choice Is Yours

We have come a long way since the beginning of time. Mankind has changed and grown and evolved and become spiritually ready for this millennium. The time has come for a new financial system to be engaged. The time has come for many changes to occur. You will see over the coming years that life as you know it will begin to unfold in a different manner. You will no longer recognize the way you do things today as something commonplace. Things will drastically change. Life as you know it will change. There is nothing to be frightened of, however, unless you choose to cling to the past as you will be held in the past. The time has come for you to move forward into this new millennium and for life to be different from how you now know it.

What will occur in the future is what has been planned for eons of time. This is an exciting time, as it's a time for which we have all been waiting. The time has come for heaven to come to earth, for man to merge with heaven. *You will see heaven on earth.* In the days to come, life will change as you know it. Clinging to the old and outmoded will only impede your progress and progress for all mankind. The time has come for all to adhere to a new standard of living. The new standard of living is one that is not new to many of you, but to many of you it is a brand new concept.

All will be judged of their own accord and all will have what they deserve because of how they live. No more will man be able to manipulate to have what he desires. What he desires will be only available to him if it is what he deserves. No man will be able to take from another. If you experience lack, it's because you believe in lack. If you believe in abundance, you will have abundance. That truly is how it exists now for many of you. However, we will go one step further in that if you are not pure at heart, you will demonstrate accordingly. The pure of heart will be the ones who have the greatest power and abundance. No more will man be able to manipulate one another or the situations within which they live. They will be judged on their purity of heart and given to accordingly.

No man will be able to manipulate God, Source of all your supply, as He can see your heart. He knows your heart like no other. He knows your essence. He knows your truth. Should you wish abundance, you should take heed that your relationship to God had better improve or your results may or may not be abundant ones.

Mankind has tried to control things long enough. With heaven coming to earth, earth and her inhabitants need to prepare and be ready for its arrival. There will be no messing around with the plans as they begin to unfold. No man will be able to interfere with what is to come. Those that resist may choose to go elsewhere. Those that are ready may stay, for the glory of God is upon them.

If you are frightened, then you should be as you must be guilty about something. Think again. Ask for forgiveness and relate to the world going forward pure in heart and do the right thing by everyone. Do not value one man over another. Do not treat one man better than another. Treat everyone equally and with respect. Recognize the divinity within each and every individual as you are all one in the Source and the Source is in each of you.

It is time for impending change. The fear that will arise is due to the lack of integrity within. Only you have the power to change that expression. Repent in order to move forward in peace. Have peace within and peace will be expressed throughout. You will be able to demonstrate exactly how you think, feel, and act. The purer your heart, the purer your results.

If you think you will be able to get away with anything, you will not. If you think you can have it all, you can. However, you need demonstrate a pure heart in order to manifest it. You manifest now out of your thoughts. You will begin to manifest out of your heart, not just your thoughts.

The time to set the record straight is now. Prepare now and the future will go more smoothly. Do nothing and nothing will change. Your results will be dictated as you now believe and behave.

The day of reckoning is upon you. It is your choice to shine or not, participate or not, rejoice or not. THE CHOICE, IS ALWAYS YOURS.

Afterword
by Michael the Archangel

Because of the timing of this transition to heaven on earth, it is imperative that mankind release karma, negative memories, and attachments and save their souls.

In light of that, Joy Pedersen has been instructed to assist the masses in their transition. She has been provided specific gifts to assist at this time. As she works with me and directly with Divinity, you can call upon her, as well as me toward that effort. She is being guided to offer programs on the physical level to assist us in this endeavor.

The following are prayers you can apply as needed and inspired:

Prayer One
Guidance and Repentance

Dear God:

Please guide me forward, during this time of transition, to walk my true path divinely guided and inspired.

Please remove from me the errors of my ways, and the thoughts and beliefs that hinder my path in the light.

May I take this moment and repent the errors of my thoughts, actions, and deeds and the negative effect they have had on animate and inanimate alike, me as well as others.

May you see my goodness and shine it with your light for all the world to see and expand your graciousness to all those in need at this time.

I am yours,

Amen

Prayer Two
For Parents

Dear God:

May I receive your guidance to make me the ideal parent to my most blessed children to inspire them to follow their true path without the influence of my intellect and memories that may eschew following the appropriate guidance.

Please release from me all harmful memories that could potentially influence my children off their divine path and help me to guide them to fill their purpose in this lifetime.

Please light our way.

Amen

Prayer Three
Release

Dear God:

May you release the cause of my pain (whether mental, physical, or emotional). I take 100% responsibility for its existence in my life. I ask your forgiveness and release so I can be free of this anguish and manifestation.

I thank you in advance for its release.

Amen

Prayer Four
Peace, Balance and Abundance

Dear God:

Please bring joy, peace, balance, and abundance to this situation or person [state situation and/or person's name].

Please God, I ask that you heal the situation.

Thank you.

Amen

Prayer Five
Redemption

Dear God:

May I redeem myself for the wrongs I have committed—known and unknown, remembered and unremembered. I turn my life over to you now and for always.

Thank you.

I love you.

Amen

Mighty Sword

I ask for Archangel Michael's mighty sword. May it cut the ties that bind me.

That is all.

Thank you.

Conclusion

Our God is a loving God, with your best interests in mind. All you need do is call upon Him in time of need and He hears your cries. It is your karma, past life memories, thoughts and beliefs that block your hearing His answers and receiving the answers to your prayers.

All the angels are here to assist you at this time as well, so call upon us for the assistance you need.

You have much support at this time.

Michael the Archangel
Your Emissary of Light

Be at peace.
Know that you are one with Me.
"I" protect you.
"I" honor you.
Stay with Me and My kingdom is yours.
Stray from Me and you may be lost to Me forever.
Know that "I" know your heart,
your motivations,
your strife and
your struggles.
"I" protect you this day forward.
If you choose Me, "I" choose you.
Do you choose Me?
"I am" the "I am", "I am" the "I"

About the Author

Joy S. Pedersen, a Licensed Spiritual Healer, Certified Spiritual Health Coach, ordained minister and Doctor of Divinity, has been employing the art of automatic writing, a form of channeling, since 1994.

Joy's path in metaphysics began when she moved to Los Angeles. During her 10 years there, she worked in the television industry, first in network publicity for Paramount Television on *Cheers, Taxi, Family Ties,* and *Happy Days,* to name a few, and completed her career as Los Angeles Bureau Chief of the syndicated magazine television show, *PM Magazine.*

It was during her time at Paramount that Joy started her business, Express Success, to help people achieve success through workshops and one-on-one consultations. She also started the first women's business network and entertainment business network while in Los Angeles. Since returning to her home state of New Jersey, she has continued her networking enterprise.

The added dimension is her experience in networking with angels and others in heaven, enabling Joy to assist others in incorporating angel guidance to fulfill their needs. Joy regularly shares messages she receives from angels and others at www.AngelEnlightenment.com.

She serves her clientele by telephone with private as well as group consultations, which are intended to bring clarity to situations and help people overcome the challenges of today affecting the areas of finance, relationships, health and wellbeing, business and career. Joy also offers coaching, tele-seminars, conventional seminars, and workshops. Joy helps individuals, as well as business owners and service professionals, with their efforts to achieve greater success and she incorporates intuitive and healing techniques to help them release problems blocking their path to greater success. The work she does to clear property, negative memories and karma from the beginning of time is helping countless people.

You can read more about Joy Pedersen and her work at www.ExpressSuccess.net.

Glossary

The following definitions are included as they relate to this particular body of work and are not to be considered complete definitions for all use:

Automatic writing – the process by which an inter-dimensional being may communicate through a form of channeling by way of the unconscious mind directly onto paper without conscious thought involved.

Blocks – any obstacle within one's psyche that inhibits desirable results.

Channel – a vehicle used by an inter-dimensional being to communicate messages to someone in another dimension.

Cleanse – to eliminate or erase negative and/or unwanted memories that contribute to less than ideal results.

Clear – to release thoughts, beliefs, obstacles, ideas, and memories that sabotage or block one's path.

Clear using ho'oponopono – using the ho'oponopono process specifically to release attachments and blocks affecting one's past or path.

Earth changes – sudden, large-scale, catastrophic natural events that include earthquakes, volcanoes, and major disturbances in weather.

Ego – the part of the self that identifies with the intellect and the perceived outer expression of life.

Ho'oponopono – a Hawaiian term meaning to correct or set aright referred to here as a spiritual process of releasing and transmuting that includes mental cleansing, repentance, and forgiveness in order to restore peace and balance.

Karma – cause and effect; for every event that occurs, there will follow another, retributive event, the existence of which was caused by the first event. The effects of negative karma include memories of wrongdoing mirrored in everything connected with all animate and inanimate objects that were present when the cause occurred, in this incarnation as well as in others.

Reincarnation – the cycle of death and rebirth. The soul or true self remains intact but is reborn in a new body to experience spiritual lessons that include working out karma.

Release – to let go, relinquish, or to set free from confinement, restraint or bondage.

Resistance – stubbornness, blockage, often psychological in nature, the act or power of resisting, opposing, or withstanding.

Further Study

If you wish to gain a deeper understanding of this material and how to apply it to your own life, you may consider forming a discussion group.

Please visit www.WisdomoftheGuardian.com for suggestions and options to further your study.

If you leave your email address at the website, you will also receive updates, as well as a free gift.